WITHDRAWN

THIRD WORLD INDUSTRIALISATION IN THE 1980s:
OPEN ECONOMIES IN A CLOSING WORLD

Third World Industrialisation in the 1980s: Open Economies in a Closing World

Edited by
RAPHAEL KAPLINSKY

FRANK CASS

First published in Great Britain by
FRANK CASS AND COMPANY LIMITED
Gainsborough House, 11 Gainsborough Road,
London E11 1RS

and in the United States of America by
FRANK CASS AND COMPANY LIMITED
c/o Biblio Distribution Centre
81 Adams Drive, P.O. Box 327, Totowa, NJ 07511

Copyright © 1984 Frank Cass & Co. Ltd.

British Library Cataloguing in Publication Data

Special issue on Third World industrialisation
in the 1980s.
1. Developing countries — Industries
1. Kaplinsky, Raphael
338.09172'4   HC59.7

ISBN 0–7146–3240–6

This group of studies first appeared in a Special Issue on
'Third World Industrialisation in the 1980s' of *The Journal
of Development Studies*, Vol. 21, No. 1, published by Frank
Cass & Co. Ltd.

*All rights reserved. No part of this publication may be repro-
duced, stored in a retrieval system, or transmitted in any
form, or by any means, electronic, mechanical, photocopy-
ing, recording, or otherwise, without the prior permission of
Frank Cass and Company Limited.*

Printed and bound in Great Britain by
T.J. Press (Padstow) Ltd, Padstow, Cornwall

218474

CONTENTS

HC
59.7
.T453
1984

EDITOR'S PREFACE

In 1957 the Russians launched the first satellite, to the consternation of the American public and the US military establishment. The response was a major expansion of technical and scientific education in the USA. If that rate of expansion had continued, then by the early 1990s there would have been 'two scientists for every man, woman, child and dog in the [US] population, and we should spend on them twice as much money as we had' [*Price*, cited in *Jahoda 1973: 211-12*]. So we should be warned about the dangers of projecting into the future on the basis of short-term historical experience.

Yet in many senses the Export-Orientated Industrialisation (EOI) strategies which are currently in vogue, reflect this process of historical projection. Based on the undoubted success of a *limited number* of Newly Industrialising Countries (NICs) over a *relatively short period of time* (about 15 years), most less developed countries are either voluntarily adopting such industrial strategies, or are being induced to do so by multi- and bi-lateral aid agencies. It is often forgotten that the export and growth success of the NICs from the mid-1960s until the end of the 1970s occurred in a time-span which, by the experience of global industrialisation, must be considered as short-run. It also took place in an historically unprecedented period of reasonably full employment in the major advanced economies, high rates of industrial growth and a virtual explosion in global trade. Besides, it also occurred within a series of social formations which were country-, temporally- and geographically-specific.

To what extent, then, can industrial strategies over the coming decade be shaped realistically by the past success of the NICs? The various contributions in this volume make no pretence of offering a viable alternative set of industrial strategies for the Third World, even if this were possible for such a heterogeneous set of class interests and countries. Rather, we have set ourselves the more limited task of questioning the viability of EOI strategies for the non-NICs, and even perhaps their maintenance for the successful NICs. In doing so the various contributions address four major sets of issues. First is a historical perspective, considering issues such as the actual experience of import-substituting industrialisation (ISI) and EOI, the flows of external finance to the Third World and the depth of industrial experience in some of the more successful NICs. Second, some attempt is made to consider the future context in which industrialisation is likely to occur, focusing on the availability of external finance, its conditionality, the advent of radical technical change, and the distortions induced on industrial development by the new cold war. Third, attention is given to the political–economic context in which industrialisation takes place; this not only addresses the implicit and explicit premises of comparative advantage-based neo-classical theories of industrialisation, but also considers the active role played by the state, particularly (but not exclusively) in socialist economies. Finally, and on a more individual note, Bob Sutcliffe reviews the intervening years since his well-known earlier book on industrialisation and reconsiders the arguments for industrialisation and in whose interests it takes place.

Inevitably there are many important areas of analysis and policy which are not confronted in any of the individual contributions in this volume. For example, there is no substantive treatment of the relationship between industry and agriculture. Similarly, the need to differentiate between different-sized economies, and even between different regions (noting the particular problems of sub-Saharan Africa) is only given passing consideration. Equally important, none of the individual contributions address themselves to the relationship between industrial strategy in individual economies and global economic recession: is global reflation a non-zero sum game offering renewed vigour to EOI strategies in the Third World? These and other important issues require careful thought before feasible industrial strategies can be charted to guide LDCs through an undoubtedly difficult period. However, it has been the editor's judgement that the more urgent issue facing LDCs has been to confront the problems arising out of the EOI strategies implicit in multilateral-aid agency conditionality. Whilst not all the individual contributions are directly addressed to this issue, it is believed that the four sets of issues outlined earlier at least provide some caveats to the adoption of such industrial strategies. At the same time, it is hoped that some insights are provided into the process of industrial accumulation in the periphery.

The birth of this collective endeavour owes much to the inspiration and support of Dudley Seers. He had planned to participate in the volume with a paper of his own, but due to his untimely death, this remained unwritten. As a colleague and a friend he was a major influence in all of our professional lives, and it is to his memory that we dedicate this volume.

REFERENCE

Jahoda, M., 1973, 'Postscript on Social Change', in H.S.D. Cole *et al.*, 1973, *Thinking about the future: A Critique of the Limits to Growth*, London: Chatto & Windus.

Industrialisation Strategies in Less Developed Countries: Some Lessons of Historical Experience

by Hubert Schmitz*

Most of the history of industrialisation in the less developed countries (LDCs) of the capitalist world has been examined under two headings: import-substituting industrialisation (ISI) and export-orientated indus- trialisation (EOI). Some of the most influential authors and policy advisers have been moving rapidly to a position of treating these experi- ences as closed chapters of development economics. The verdict is that ISI has not worked (or only in its early stages) and that EOI under liberal policies has been so successful that LDCs in general should follow this route. Our argument is that ISI has indeed led to substantial (static) inefficiency and foreign exchange problems, but that from a dynamic perspective the analyses are still most unsatisfactory – for both conceptual and empirical reasons. Second, we suggest that the alleged superiority of EOI is not so much due to the adoption of more 'rational' market-orientated policies, but due to a combination of cyclical and historical factors and to substantial discriminatory state intervention. The paper concludes with some reflections on industrialisation strategies for the 1980s.

I: THE DISENCHANTMENT WITH IMPORT–SUBSTITUTING INDUSTRIALISATION (ISI) – JUSTIFIED OR PREMATURE?

The *economic* arguments for ISI and protection have a long and disting- uished history. In the early LDC literature, ISI was seen as a prerequisite for halting the transfer of surplus from the periphery to the centre [*ECLA, 1950; Prebisch, 1959*]. Given the division of labour between central and peripheral economies, the distribution of gains from international trade and technolo- gical progress were said to be uneven. Rapid industrialisation under at least temporary protection was seen as the way out. Another body of economic arguments centred more on internal dynamic factors such as learning by doing and externalities.[1] This thinking has once again become prevalent in recent analyses which emphasise that ISI must include a certain degree of local capital goods production [*Rosenberg, 1976; Stewart, 1976*]. But there are prominent historical precedents; most notably Friedrich List's [*1841*] theory of productive forces which he put forward to present a front against the theory of comparative advantage. To him, developing productive forces meant building up domestic coherent economic circuits; to achieve this the

* Institute of Development Studies at the University of Sussex. Comments from Fabio Erber, David Evans, Martin Godfrey, Raphie Kaplinsky, Richard Luedde-Neurath and Sheila Smith are gratefully acknowledged, but the views expressed here are not necessarily shared by them.

infant economy had to be protected from the world economy; a strong nation state was thought necessary to achieve temporary seclusion. The *political* argument for ISI is summed up in the desire for greater self-sufficiency and independence.

Yet it seems that much of the initial ISI, particularly in Latin America, was not fuelled by the economic or political rationale. The common stance in the literature is that early ISI did *not* result from *consciously adopted* policies but was *externally enforced* [e.g. *Hirschman, 1968; Ballance et al., 1982*]. International circumstances prevailing in the period 1914–45 are the most frequently cited explanation for the emergence of ISI in LDCs. Two world wars and an interim depression made continued importation of industrial goods difficult, or even impossible, because earnings from exporting primary commodities fell, and/or because the nations at war were unable to supply industrial goods. That this sparked off a major wave of industrialisation is indeed plausible and of course compatible with dependency theory (most notably Frank [*1971*]); but also those analyses and surveys which are not in the dependency tradition underwrite this position [e.g. *Little, Scitovsky and Scott, 1970*]. Unfortunately this assertion is poorly documented and rarely given more than one or two paragraphs. Even more sobering is the fact that economic historians find it difficult to support this view of externally enforced ISI; in fact some cast doubt on its empirical validity [*Dean, 1969; Villela and Suzigan, 1977; Ingham and Simmons, 1981; Miller, 1981; Albert and Henderson, 1981*].

Our point is not to argue against the view that industrialisation in the periphery surges ahead during crises in the centre, but to call for recognition that in the first half of this century the connection is far from clear. Since we are concerned with the international context for national industrial strategies and since the central economies are at present undergoing their second major economic crisis in this century (even though not identical to the first), this is an uncomfortable lacuna in the map of knowledge.

Import-substitution achieved from the 1950s onwards was more a result of deliberate economic policies. The main device used was the restriction of imports of manufactured goods in the form of tariffs, quotas and multiple exchange rates. Their use however was not always aimed at industrialisation as such, but was often a response to balance of payments difficulties. The measures adopted and the results have been subjected to considerable scrutiny, particularly for the decades of the 1950s and 1960s. The data show that considerable advances were made in the degree of industrialisation; the share of manufacturing in GDP increased and the share of imports in total domestic supply was lowered significantly. The overwhelming conclusion, however, was one of disenchantment, even in the structuralist quarters of ECLA, which had hitherto been among the main advocates of ISI [see e.g. *Prebish, 1964; Tavares, 1964*]. The critique emerged from many country and sector studies, the main results of which were drawn together in surveys by Hirschman [*1968*], Bruton [*1970*], Baer [*1972*], Sutcliffe [*1971*], Diaz-Alejandro [*1975*], Donges [*1976*] and Nixson [*1982*]. The most influential attack on ISI came from a comparative study by Little, Scitovsky and Scott

[*1970*], the gist of which is worth recalling. The main argument is that protection was overdone and led to an inefficient allocation of resources due to distortions in factor and product markets. More specifically their critique was directed against the following:

(1) *Instrinsic problems of government interference.* Excessive administrative regulations gave rise to bureaucratisation, corruption, uncertainty and delays and thus discouraged productive private initiative.

(2) *Bias against exports.* The existence of import restrictions led to a higher exchange rate than would have prevailed under a free trade regime, reducing the relative gains obtained from exporting.

(3) *Bias against agriculture.* The protection of local industry raised the prices of manufactured goods relative to agricultural products in the home market and the overvalued exchange rate reduced the domestic currency receipts for agricultural exports.

(4) *Under-utilisation of installed capacity.* Since import controls did not equally apply to capital goods and since credit for installing machinery was relatively cheap, factories were over-equipped. Moreover protection in product markets made it possible to earn good profits even at low capacity utilisation.

(5) *Under-utilisation of labour.* Capital goods could be obtained relatively cheaply due to the combined effect of over-valued exchange rates, low import restrictions for such goods and subsidised financing conditions, resulting in a bias against employment of labour.

(6) *Import intensity of ISI.* While the importation of consumer goods was reduced substantially, this was achieved at the expense of increased imports of equipment and materials, resulting – contrary to expectations – in an even more rigid dependence on foreign supplies and renewed foreign exchange crises.

(7) *The slowing down of ISI.* Although initially industry can grow faster than domestic demand for manufactures, LDCs soon run out of import substitution possibilities. After that growth rates can only be maintained by a growth in domestic demand or in exports; but by then the structure and inefficiency of industry stand in the way of conquering export markets.

The policy implications drawn from this analysis were that government interference should be reduced, the free play of market forces should be encouraged, tariffs and quotas should be lowered substantially and exchange rates should be devalued. Where domestic industry suffered disadvantages (that is, private cost higher than social cost), subsidies should be given rather than protection from foreign competition. Such policies would bring the country's productive structure in line with comparative advantage and pave the way for an outward-looking policy. This in a nutshell is the neo-classical position on ISI. While most observers can agree with most of the empirical findings of the underlying studies,[2] agreement with the policy recommendations does not necessarily follow. Indeed, the analysts who can be loosely grouped together under the dependency school argue not for less state intervention but for more and of a more fundamental kind.

The different stance on policy comes from an analysis which endogenises the state and sees the distorted and inefficient productive structure (documented in such detail by neo-classical and some structuralist authors) as a result of the colonial heritage and of social class formation and economic control mechanisms which emerged in the neo-colonial period. The main arguments which can be filtered out of the various dependency writings [e.g. *Merhav, 1969; Sunkel, 1973; Cardoso and Faletto, 1970; Vaitsos, 1974; Thomas, 1974*] are:

(1) ISI accepted the pattern of demand and the underlying distribution of income (inherited from the past) as given, whereas it would have been necessary to alter radically consumption patterns and distributional profiles.

(2) ISI encouraged foreign penetration of the economy; in particular the establishment of subsidiaries of international firms behind tariff barriers led to the elimination of many local producers and rendered the industrial structure monopolistic.

(3) ISI meant the incorporation of technologies from advanced countries which were inappropriate to local conditions and led to heavy outflow of capital in the form of transfer pricing, royalty payments, and so on.

(4) ISI resulted in the protected accumulation of the indigenous bourgeoisie in alliance with (or subordinated to) international capital.

(5) The overall effect of ISI was one of transnational integration and national disintegration of the economy and society.

Hence the solution cannot lie in a greater reliance on market forces, but in more radical promotion of national or regional industrial policies which include greater control of foreign enterprises, greater scrutiny over imports of technology, reform of the tax and incentive system and redistribution of income. In other words, these are policies which may require more fundamental political change, aimed at a different kind of inward-looking strategy.[3]

Even though the policy conclusions emerging from these critiques are very different, the analyses themselves are to some extent complementary. As noted by Nixson [*1982*] most of the empirical findings of the neo-classical critique could be incorporated into a broadly based dependency view. Despite these differences it is clear that there was a widespread disillusion with ISI right across the ideological and analytical spectrum.

In its economic dimension, the alleged failure of ISI is summed up in the low efficiency of industry reflected in the high cost of its output. Since efficiency is a relative concept, performance in any activity must be defined in relation to some alternative. The most obvious point of comparison is the cost of importing the product in question. In this sense, the nominal rate of protection which indicates the percentage by which the domestic price can exceed the world market price can be a rudimentary measure of the ineffi-

TABLE 1

AVERAGE EFFECTIVE RATES OF PROTECTION (ERP) IN
MANUFACTURING INDUSTRY OF LESS DEVELOPED COUNTRIES

Country	Year	ERP	Country	Year	ERP
Argentina	1958	162*	Jamaica	1978	50
	1977	38	Kenya	1967	92
Brazil	1966	118*	Korea (South)	1968	-1
	1967	66	Malaysia	1963	-8
	1980/81	46		1970	38
Chile	1961	190	Mexico	1960	27*
	1967	217		1970	49
Colombia	1969	29	Nicaragua	1968	53
	1979	44	Nigeria	1968	99
Costa Rica	1968	22	Pakistan	1963	271*
Dominican Rep.	1971	124		1970/71	181
Egypt	1956	55	Philippines	1965	63
	1966/67	42		1974	59
El Salvador	1968	44	Singapore	1967	6
Ghana	1968/70	143	South Africa	1963/64	17
Guatemala	1968	31	Sri Lanka	1970	118
Honduras	1968	59	Sudan	1971	179
India	1961	313*	Taiwan	1966	44
	1968/69	125	Tanzania	1966	116
Indonesia	1971	101	Thailand	1969	16
Iran	1967	75	Uruguay	1968	384
Israel	1958	46	LDC average	1966-72	72
	1968	71			
Ivory Coast	1970/72	72			

Sources: (1) Most of the data were taken from O. Havrylyshyn and I. Alikhani, 'Protection Levels and Policies in Developing and Industrial Countries – Annotated Bibliography and Data Bank Summary', mimeo, International Trade Division, Economic Analysis Department, The World Bank, Washington, D.C., 1982. Permission to utilise parts of the data gathered in this document is gratefully acknowledged.
(2) Those figures which carry an asterisk are taken from I. Little, T. Scitovsky and M. Scott, *Industry and Trade in Some Developing Countries*, Oxford University Press for OECD, 1970.

ciency of local producers. A more meaningful indicator – even though more difficult to calculate – is the effective rate of protection [*Corden, 1971; Balassa, 1971*]; it shows the percentage increase in *value added* afforded by protection over the value added which would prevail in a non-protected situation. The many country studies carried out in the 1960s and 1970s

revealed levels of protection substantially higher than those ever enjoyed by
the now developed countries [e.g. *Little, Scitovsky and Scott, 1970; Balassa
et al., 1971*]. Since one can assume that most of this protection was actually
used by LDC producers (that is, not entirely redundant), Table 1 provides a
general picture of the magnitude of inefficiency as measured by effective
rates of protection.[4]

Evidence of the kind presented in Table 1 is now amply available and
indeed important. At best, however, these indicators can provide a picture
of the *static* inefficiency of industry in LDCs. It is remarkable how little this
industrial performance has been investigated from a *dynamic* perspective.
Most accounts remind us of the importance of learning-by-doing and external economies to industrial growth; but in the actual evaluation these
considerations simply evaporate. In a way this is not surprising in a discipline
in which so often difficulties in quantification have led to neglecting the
question altogether. After all, our conceptual apparatus to disentangle the
dynamic changes is weak, not to speak of the problem of operationalising
concepts for the purpose of measuring. Krueger's [*1981:7*] query on whether
the dynamic factors should be expected to unfold at the sectoral or national
level serves as a reminder of the conceptual problems:

> In terms of assessing import-substitution policies as a strategy with which
> to confer inducements to infant industries, it is important to note that the
> theory of infant industry itself is ambiguous in indicating what the source
> of the dynamic factor might be: on the one hand, if such dynamic factors
> are specific to particular industries such as glass-blowing or electronics,
> then the number of industries which should receive infant industry pro-
> tection at any given time should be relatively small. If, on the other hand,
> externalities and dynamic cost reductions are a function of the size of the
> entire industrial sector, then inducements to produce should be fairly
> uniform across industrial activities, as the same dynamic benefits would
> accrue regardless of the precise industries which were growing rapidly.

List's [*1841*] theory of productive forces encompasses both an infant industry and an infant economy argument.[5] Recent attempts to come to terms
with the dynamic factors have been primarily of an industry-specific or even
firm-specific kind. Bell [*1982*] has reviewed the existing empirical evidence.
The upshot is that learning in infant enterprises and industries has been
highly variable; common characteristics of the maturation path of industries
do not emerge, neither on the duration of infancy nor on the magnitude of its
costs. The weight of the evidence suggests, however, that relatively pro-
tracted maturation periods and correspondingly high infancy costs are more
common. When the firms or industries are set in their differing contexts
some pattern seems to emerge. The more successful learners tend to come
from LDCs with a relatively long industrialisation experience stretching
back to at least the 1920s (e.g. Argentina, Brazil or India). Much of the
evidence on low rates of progress is drawn from economies in which significant industrialisation only began in the 1950s (e.g. Bangladesh, Thailand or
Tanzania). However, Bell [*1982*] warns not to make too much of the difference of three decades of industrial development because the total number of

cases studied is small and because there is no reason to believe that the case studies are in any way representative of the experience in the different types of economy.

Assessing dynamic efficiency at the macro-level is even more problematic, but no less important. It would require capturing not only advances in the learning process but also the development of externalities and linkages over time. Thus a set of micro-economically less efficient activities (considered individually) may produce a macro-economically efficient result through developing linkages and externalities; conversely, micro-economically efficient activities may produce a macro-economic relative inefficiency. The concept of dynamic efficiency also suggests that industrialisation as it proceeds opens up new areas of productive activity in which local labour can henceforth be employed at levels of productivity which are relatively high due to already existing or emerging linkages and externalities [*Bienefeld, 1982c*]. For instance, Schmitz [*1982*] links the potential of *evolutionary* growth in small-scale manufacturing to the existence of a *local* technological infrastructure consisting of machine-makers, suppliers of spare parts and second-hand equipment, and small engineering firms which can repair or copy parts. The evidence for this argument of externalities is merely suggestive and not conclusive. Indeed, in general the evidence on externalities is slight and unsystematic. As Cooper and Hoffman [*1981: 26*] conclude, 'the lack of empirical knowledge makes it difficult to say how and where the state should intervene. At present these externality arguments are part of a case for technological protectionism, but how much protectionism, in what form and directed to what particular types of technology is impossible to say'.

Thus the concern with dynamic efficiency takes us rapidly to the question of protection of technologies or import substitution of technological capability. This has become almost a separate field of investigation over the last 15 years and Erber [*1983*] provides a useful reassessment of the different ways in which advances (or lack of them) in building up indigenous technological capability have been examined. An essential part of the technological capacity is a local capital goods sector. Considerable progress has been achieved in expanding this sector; in fact in a good number of LDCs its rate of growth has been faster than that of industry as a whole. The degree of import substitution achieved so far varies enormously. At the top end are China, India and Brazil (in descending order) which have already achieved domestic supply ratios which are in the order of 75 to over 90 per cent and similar to those of the advanced industrial nations; but in the majority of LDCs, less than a third of capital goods has a domestic origin [*UNCTAD, 1982*].[6]

As in the case of consumption goods, the import substitution of capital goods can be achieved by restricting the import of the final product, but an increase in the domestic supply ratio of capital goods would be a limited (though not meaningless) indicator of indigenous technological capacity, if there were a mere replication of the formerly imported (often inappropriate) machinery and equipment. Yet copying imported designs has been dominant. For the individual firm it is almost always easier and cheaper to import well-tried designs from abroad than to invest in the creation of indigenous design capabilities. Hence the widespread concern to develop policies towards imported technology whether embodied in machines, paper (for example, designs) or people (for example, engineers). There is widespread agreement that where the inflow of technology is uninhibited, the local capability for research, design and project execution develops more slowly. It is also agreed that keeping all technology imports out would be absurd since the countries concerned would have to re-invent everything. Much valuable local technological activity takes the form of learning from imported technology and from adapting and modifying it. The serious arguments are about the extent to which protection is necessary and what additional policies are required [e.g. *Cooper, 1980; Dahlman and Westphal, 1982; UNCTAD, 1982*].

In this context it is generally held that much can be learnt from Japan's successful policy of selected technology imports (often for purposes of reverse engineering) combined with substantial and strategically applied local R & D. However, the lessons from policies adopted in LDCs are more ambiguous; compare for example India and Brazil. India has long pursued policies of protecting local technological efforts, whereas Brazil has relied more on technology brought in by international firms or on continuous licensing. India has arguably achieved a greater import substitution of technological *know-how* and *know-why* [*Lall, 1982*], but its overall industrial performance has not kept up with that of Brazil.

Most importantly, research on these questions is growing rapidly. In essence, the recent and burgeoning literature on indigenous technological capability [e.g. in *Stewart and James (eds.), 1982*; or in *Fransman and King (eds.), forthcoming*] is nothing but a belated recognition of mainstream economics that the dynamic factors must be given more thought in devising and assessing industrialisation strategies, particularly if they are inward-looking. It is quite conceivable that this will eventually lead to a more qualified assessment of ISI which has hitherto so often been labelled a failure. Below we will also ask to what extent ISI laid the foundation for the apparent success of strategies geared to the promotion of exports.

II: THE SUCCESS OF EXPORT-ORIENTATED INDUSTRIALISATION (EOI): RESULT OF THE 'RIGHT' POLICIES?

The verdict of the failure of ISI gained force when an alternative emerged which showed all the signs of success. Countries which had switched emphasis during the 1960s to export-oriented industrialisation achieved the most remarkable rates of economic growth. They soon became called the Newly Industrialised Countries (NICs) and their record became the main theme of the industrialisation debate of the 1970s and early 1980s.

The literature does not always apply the term NICs to the same countries. Most lists include South Korea, Taiwan, Hong Kong, Singapore, Brazil and, less frequently, Mexico;[7] these are the countries which are generally referred to in this section. Together they accounted for 62 per cent of LDC manufactured exports in 1975 [*Lall, 1980*]. The first five, the 'arch NICs', achieved annual growth rates of GDP (at constant prices) of between eight and 11 per cent over the period 1965–78;[8] their yearly increases in manufactured exports lay between 20 and 40 per cent.[9] This expansion did not fail to leave its impact on the labour market. Manufacturing employment in that period increased by between four and eight per cent yearly,[10] leading in some regions of those countries (and in some years) to labour shortages and real wage increases.

The performance of these NICs is impressive by any standards.[11] The question is what factors account for this success. The dominant explanation (emerging from mainstream economics) is that these countries adopted the 'right' policies, by liberalising imports, adopting 'realistic' exchange rates and providing incentives for exports; above all they managed to get factor prices right so that their economies could expand in line with their comparative advantage; reliance on market forces and integration into the world economy yield results superior to protection and dissociation from the world economy [*Balassa, 1978, 1981; Bhagwati, 1978; Krueger, 1978; Donges, 1976*]. For instance, Tyler [*1976: 278*] attributes Brazil's boom to 'a general tendency to rationalise, i.e., liberalise, economic policy around the price system'. Westphal [*1978: 375*] concludes that 'Korea provides an almost classical example of an economy following its comparative advantage and reaping the gains predicted by conventional economic theory'; and Little [*1981: 42*], in an assessment of the Asian NICs and of the possibilities of emulation, concludes 'The major lesson is that labour intensive export-oriented policies, which amounted to almost free trade conditions for exporters, were the prime cause of an extremely rapid and labour intensive industrialisation ...'

This interpretation of the rise of the NICs has come under attack. Thus Bienefeld [*1982a, 1982b, 1983*] argues strongly against characterising the NICs as the 'embodiment of the neo-classical parable' and puts forward an alternative view. The emergence of the NICs is seen as a response to a set of international circumstances which at one and the same time produced relatively favourable access to markets of advanced countries, dramatically increased access to international finance and increasing relocation of production by transnational corporations (TNCs) to the periphery. These factors are seen as having conditioned the emergence of the NICs but not as having determined which countries would seize the opportunities. The view is that this was determined partly by location and geo-political significance; partly by the existence of a strong (repressive) internationally reliable regime; and partly by the existence of a technological infrastructure resulting from earlier import-substitution policies. Finally, state control over industrial development is held to be extensive and decisive in bringing about the dynamic growth.

This and several other contributions in this volume tend to support this view; in some respects the arguments are further strengthened, in others they are qualified. Let us take them up one by one. To what extent was the expansion of exports attributable to the *locational decisions of TNCs*? The movement of factories (as opposed to merely capital) from the centre to the periphery accelerated from the mid-1960s onwards as a result of various factors: declining profitability in advanced countries; increasing competition between them (especially with the appearance of Japan as a major competitor on world markets); rising wages in Europe and North America; and increasing difficulties in maintaining control over labour at the site of production. The actual relocation was facilitated by advances made in transport and communication technology and by increased fragmentation of jobs: complex tasks were decomposed into simple tasks such that workers with only little training could achieve high levels of productivity. Simultaneously a number of LDCs, most notably the NICs offered a docile, cheap labour force and generous incentives in the form of tax exemption or subsidised infrastructure, culminating in a growing number of Export Processing Zones. Under these conditions the relocation of production became an irresistible, in some cases unavoidable, move for producers in the advanced countries [*NACLA, 1975; Fröbel et al., 1977; Bienefeld et al., 1977; Spiegel, 1980; Joekes, 1982*].

None of this is to say that foreign capital became less interested in the internal markets of LDCs. The argument is about external markets: a significant proportion of the increased LDCs' exports came to be carried out by foreign subsidiaries or by local producers which were subcontracted by foreign manufacturers or trading houses. Systematic data on the extent of international subcontracting hardly exist but some indications of the proportion of exports accounted for by foreign majority-owned enterprises can be given. Nayyar [*1978*] pieced together information from various sources which showed that the share of TNCs in exports of NICs were: Hong Kong, 10 per cent (1972); South Korea, at least 15 per cent (1971); Taiwan, at least 20 per cent (1971); Singapore, nearly 70 per cent (1970); Brazil, 43 per cent (1969); Mexico, 25-30 per cent (1970). A similar exercise carried out later by Lall [*1980*] suggests a more important TNC role: South Korea, 31 per cent (1974); Singapore, 84 per cent (1975); Brazil, 51 per cent (1973); Mexico, 34 per cent (1974). Export shares of TNCs differ widely between industrial branches. They tend to be highest in the export of machinery, electric and electronic equipment (generally well over 60 per cent) and low in the traditional exports of textiles, clothing and shoes, but it is precisely in the latter that international subcontracting of local producers is known to be more common, even though comprehensive quantitative information is not available [*Lall, 1980; Helleiner, 1981; Germidis, 1981*].

Thus the degree and manner in which LDCs became locations for world market production controlled by international capital varied between countries and branches, but clearly formed part of the context for their expansion of exports.[12] Manufactured exports were allowed into Europe and North American markets without major obstacles, since these economies were still in their post-war boom (which was soon to come to an end). Most of them had introduced special 'value-added tariffs' which facilitated the farming out of part of the production process to low wage countries. Their exact provision varied from country to country, but they all permitted manufactured articles to enter national markets partially free of tariff duties when raw materials have originated in the country of importation. In the case of the US, imports from LDCs under these tariffs (items 807.00 and 806.30) rose by 29.5 per cent annually between 1966 and 1979. The largest share came from

Mexico, followed by Taiwan, Singapore, Hong Kong and Malaysia. For most of the 1970s, their exports under this tariff provision rose more quickly than their total manufactured exports to the US [*Helleiner, 1981*]. Finally, the favourable market conditions for export promotion policies at that time are perhaps best underlined by the rapid expansion of world trade; growth rates of international trade peaked to an exceptional 18 per cent per year between 1967 and 1973.[13] These were exactly the years in which the NICs scored their greatest successes.

The international context for the rise of the NICs was further favoured by their easy access to finance. A buoyant transnational banking market developed over the 1960s and 1970s, specialising in borrowing and lending of currencies outside the country of issue, commonly known as the 'Euro-dollar' market.[14] In the 1960s the currency supply was fuelled mainly by US balance of payments deficits (caused in particular by massive military and related expenditure abroad during the Vietnam War) and in the 1970s by the surpluses of the oil-exporting countries: the private transnational banks became the main conduit for recycling these 'petro dollars'. Credit from these banks expanded extremely rapidly between 1966 and 1978 (over 50 times) and by the end of the 1970s over 50 per cent of loans had gone to LDCs. The largest borrowers were the NICs with Mexico, Brazil, South Korea and the Philippines accounting for over 50 per cent of total accumulated debt to transnational banks in 1980 [*Griffith-Jones, 1980, 1982*].

Access to this private capital market allowed countries which obtained large volumes of credit to avoid the influence of IMF conditionality on economic policy. Most importantly, they were able to sustain levels of imports well above those they could have afforded if such loans had not been available. Dell and Lawrence [*1980*] have shown that those countries which maintained their imports also maintained high growth rates of both investment and output. Brazil provides a textbook example of an economy which was able to keep up its high growth rates through a strategy of 'debt-led growth'. The article by Griffith-Jones and Rodriguez in this volume explores this question, highlighting what difference the access to the transnational private capital market made to the growth record of various groups of developing countries.

In the 1970s the poorest countries were unable to follow the example of the NICs and finance their balance of payments deficits by external private capital flows. As a result their capacity to import declined. As indicated in the 1981 *World Development Report*, during the 1970s per capita growth in the poorest countries decreased substantially in comparison with their achievements in the 1960s (or with that of the NICs in the 1970s); most disturbing was the evolution in the poorest countries of sub-Saharan Africa where average GNP per capita actually declined by 0.4 per cent annually. While many factors contributed to this deterioration, constraints on their capacity to import played a major role, and larger external finance would have helped to achieve a better performance, particularly in industry.

The favourable external context is only part of an alternative interpretation of the rise of the NICs. Amongst the internal factors, the actual role played by the state is the first and perhaps most important to be analysed. It seems that with the exception of Hong Kong and possibly Singapore, the NICs were not the liberal, market-orientated economies they appeared to be. In the South Korean case, for example, import restrictions were reduced selectively and gradually suggesting an awareness on the part of the state that liberalisation must reflect the competitive strength of the evolving local producers. Restrictions on direct foreign investment were (and continue to be) extensive; and industrial policy has been strongly reminiscent of Japan with major decisions taken on the basis of longer-term objectives and in disregard of short-term efficiency as indicated by existing prices. In general the state has played an active and central role in the allocation of resources [*Datta-Chauduri, 1981; Bienefeld, 1982b*].Indeed

> with tight discretionary control over investment and export decisions able to be exerted via the capital market, the government could afford to establish a set of relatively liberal foreign trading policies. The neo-classical focus on the link between trading policies and growth has thus been misleading, for it has obscured the significance of capital market controls as means of state direction of economic activity [*Wade, 1982: 146-7*].

Datta-Chauduri [*1981*] suggests that the government directly or indirectly controlled the allocation of more than two-thirds of the investible resources. A study by Luedde-Neurath [*1983*] further clarifies what happened on the trade front, emphasising that Korea's export-oriented development success was neither preceded nor accompanied by significant across-the-board import liberalisation and that market forces were *not* given a free reign to allocate resources.[15] Instead there was a two-pronged import policy: liberal towards inputs for export manufacturing and highly restrictive towards the domestic market. Moreover there was a tendency to 'cross-tie' the domestic and the export market by making access to the (protected and hence profit-able) domestic market conditional upon satisfactory export performance. Overall it is concluded that 'the Korean import regime has been highly "managed" throughout the last two decades' [*Luedde-Neurath, 1983: 7*].

In the case of Taiwan, too, the state has pursued an active, selective interventionist role [*Hamilton, 1983*], but the issue is comparatively little explored. In the Latin American NICs state intervention has perhaps not been quite as strategic as in South Korea, but nevertheless extensive. Thus it is hard to agree with Balassa's [*1981: 12*] conclusion that the 'countries applying outward-oriented development strategies ... provided for auto-maticity and stability in the incentive system ... minimised price distortions and relied on the market mechanism for efficient resource allocation and rapid economic growth'. The paper by Evans and Alizadeh below explicitly takes on the question of market-determined factor prices versus state con-trol. They criticise in particular the neo-classical account of wage determina-tion in the NICs which emphasises the elimination of state intervention inimicable to a market determination of the wage and which abstracts from the political control of labour exercised by capital and the state. In general they conclude that the NICs reveal far less reliance on the invisible hand guided by enlightened market-orientated economic policy than is portrayed in the neo-classical interpretation.

Let us continue with the internal factors which contributed to the growth performance of the NICs. An analysis of the Brazilian case would point to important *internal cyclical features*. In the years immediately prior to the explosive growth of GNP and exports, industrial capacity in Brazil was heavily underutilised. 'The existence of idle productive capacity in the manufacturing sector was not the reason *why* output growth took place, but was the single most important condition that permitted the boom' [*Malan and Bonelli, 1977: 22*]. Until the early 1970s output was able to grow at a faster rate than did the stock of capital, and only then did manufacturing *investment* accelerate significantly in response to continuing internal and external demand pressing upon productive capacity. In the assessment of the other NICs there is little concern with internal economic cycles, so it is difficult to judge how general the coincidence of liberalisation experience and upturn in cycle was. However, if idle capacity was such a recurring feature under ISI as generally argued, the availability of this capacity must have helped those economies which then tried to speed up their growth under the export banner.

This takes us to a more general question, namely to what extent was ISI a precondition for successful export-led growth and how much sense does it therefore make to juxtapose the two as alternatives. To the extent that the increase in exports is achieved by outward *processing*, previous ISI is probably of little importance, as can be judged by the ease with which production facilities were relocated around the globe in the 1960s and 1970s. But, as observed above, only part of the expansion of exports took this form and the following reflections are about export manufacturing which is more 'indigenised'.

The problem is that it is inherently difficult to produce evidence which shows that protection under ISI generated externalities and learning which would have been lost without it. But it may not be accidental that some of the successful exporters were countries in which import substitution was relatively successful in building up an industrial structure which was not merely limited to local production of consumer goods. The most notable case is Brazil which also had its fair share of inefficient producers, but the degree of vertical integration achieved under ISI was such that Baer [*1965: 142*] concluded, 'The picture which emerges ... from the simultaneous growth of industries which to a large extent are each other's customers is that of a remarkably balanced growth ... many complementary industries grew up simultaneously and acted as self-reinforcing factors.'

The importance of significant industrialisation prior to the export expansion phase has also been stressed in the case of South Korea. According to Datta-Chaudhuri [*1981: 52*] 'an impressive structure of manufacturing industries, supported by an adequate infrastructure of transport and communication was inherited from the Japanese'. Even though the Korean war led to considerable destruction, it did not destroy the accumulated industrial experience, technical skills and entrepreneurship which developed between the 1920s and 1940s (see Evans and Alizadeh in this volume). A modified version of this argument could also be extended to Taiwan and Hong Kong. Although there was not the same degree of prior industrialisation as in South Korea, there was a considerable influx of people with technical and entrepreneurial abilities from mainland China [*Lee, 1981*]. Singapore is an exception, but it relied so heavily on foreign capital that its case is consistent with the above argument.

These observations relating to the South Asian countries underline the importance of accumulating industrial experience for success in export manufacturing, but are not sufficient to make the case for ISI as a precondition for EOI. Indeed one has to recognise that (by the time the export boom began) ISI in the East Asian countries was not as 'deep' as in the case of their Latin American counterparts. The latter had already moved much further into the production of consumer durables, intermediate and capital goods, yet the former were even more successful in their export expansion [*Ranis, 1981*].

Clearly there is no easy answer to our question. It is even more complicated because some of the NICs pursued a combined strategy of export promotion in some sectors and import substitution in others. Both Korea and Brazil, for example, made remarkable progress during the 1970s in building up their capital goods industries through protective measures. This gives rise to doubts about how much sense it makes to present ISI and EOI as practical alternatives. One must certainly wonder how meaningful/justified it is to use the NICs' experience to proclaim that 'export promotion outperforms import substitution' [*Krueger, 1981: 5*].

Summing up, our intention is not to dispute the growth performance of the NICs, even though it is worth remembering that many accounts of these success stories tend to forget that some of this growth (especially that arising from export processing) has generated an industry whose survival is unstable, which has few linkages with the rest of the economy and which has resulted in little transfer of know-how and skills. Rather our main concern is the explanation of the remarkable growth experiences. Without doubt the partial dismantling of import restrictions, exchange-rate adjustments and export incentives contributed to the success of these economies. However, liberalisation in one sphere cannot be taken as an indicator of increased reliance on market forces. Moreover, the policy changes led to immediate[16] and spectacular results because of favourable national and, particularly, international developments of a largely cyclical nature. Their relative importance varied between the NICs, but hopefully this and other contributions in this volume can help to redress the balance in the interpretation of this dynamic growth. This is all the more important because the NICs have been turned into model economies whose 'rational' economic policies other LDCs are advised to follow.

III: INDUSTRIALISATION STRATEGIES IN THE 1980s

The main argument in our previous section was that the success of EOI in the NICs cannot be attributed primarily to export-orientated policy changes.

Our emphasis on cyclical and historical factors in the analysis of the past itself throws doubt on the possibility of generalising EOI strategies to different times and places. However, even if one accepted the dominant neo-classical position, we believe that there are serious obstacles to the NICs maintaining their success in export expansion and even more so for other countries emulating them. The first problem lies in the fallacy of composition, whereby what works for a limited number of countries does not work if it is adopted by the large majority. Cline [*1982*], in a careful simulation exercise has analysed the consequences of a generalisation of the East Asian model of export-led development across all LDCs. His conclusion is that 'it would result in untenable market penetration into industrial countries' (p. 88).

Other obstacles lie in the changed conditions of the world economy in the 1980s. Kaplinsky's article in this volume analyses how these affect the prospects for industrial growth in the LDCs: first, rising protectionism in the advanced countries discriminates most severely against LDC manufactures. Second, the new micro electronics-based technologies tend to undermine the comparative advantage of LDC producers. Third, the high indebtedness of LDCs and increased importance of the IMF and World Bank as sources of external finance may lead to de-industrialisation, thus threatening the long-run viability of any industrial strategy. The main argument is that a generalised commitment to EOI is misplaced. This message is also echoed in Singh's [*1983*] analysis of the international context for industrialisation. He singles out the 'beggar-my-neighbour competitive deflation' as the main obstacle to EOI. With advanced and less developed countries attempting to achieve a balance on their payments by deflating their economies, they push each other into deficit and the net outcome is a vicious circle of deflation, reduced import capacity and shrinking international trade.

For these reasons LDCs are unlikely to find the dynamic for industrial growth outside, in the world economy. By implication a greater emphasis on inward looking strategies is needed, even though this is not equally compelling or feasible for all countries. First, one must distinguish between the NICs and other LDCs. While the export potential of the NICs is also affected by the changing international forces, they have a greater capacity to respond by shifting their market targetting or sectoral emphasis.[17] Second, the size of the economy plays a role; small ones have to engage more than large ones in trade and specialisation for industrial development. Irrespective of size, many LDCs do need to maintain or increase their foreign exchange earnings in order to finance essential imports. But this does not mean that industrial policy must be dominated by the drive to penetrate international markets for manufactures. Indeed, stressing the hostile international environment does not constitute an argument against the striving for exports, but calls for recognition that this is increasingly costly and that the pursuit of more inward-looking strategies may offer greater potential:

> in the coming decade the countries of the South will have to rely much more on their internal dynamics, on the growth of internal demand, rather than on world market forces to generate economic expansion.

> They will need greater import substitution, more internal technological
> development and more economic and technical cooperation among
> themselves [*Singh 1983: 25*].

This has, of course, been tried in the past. We have summarised above the
main problems encountered in the pursuit of ISI. Erber [*1983*] highlights
why indigenous technological development has been limited even in
relatively advanced Third World countries; and Vaitsos [*1978*] has undertaken a wide-ranging review of why attempts at industrial and technological
cooperation or integration between LDCs have not been all that successful.
The problem of doing better in future is political rather than technical or
economic. Take, for instance, the question of technical choice under ISI.
There are many instances in which alternative types of industrial investment
are available (the so-called appropriate technologies) which would not
display the adverse operating characteristics which condemn the existing
industry to inefficiency. Yet these appropriate technologies are being systematically excluded *not* because they are unviable but because they do not
reflect the dominant interests which seek accumulation via links with foreign
firms.[18] Thus, calling for greater inward orientation and self-reliance must
not blind us to the dangers that in practice this will be misused; that it will not
represent an expression of positive nationalism, but a smoke-screen for
narrow interests which make their links with the international economy at
the expense of 'national development'.

The need to re-examine the case for inward-looking industrialisation and
the political conditions which make these feasible inevitably throws up the
question of the socialist alternative. This is where White's contribution to
this volume is so important. He not only brings out the substantial growth
which socialist countries achieved under strong state direction; he also
underlines the very contradictions which emerge in the process of industrial
growth and sophistication of the economy. Too often the strong state
required to get purposeful industrialisation under way, becomes 'a bastion
of economic irrationality and political authoritarianism'[19] (White in this
volume).

Unfortunately every change begins from the place one is at now – and
therefore choices are massively constrained by the legacies of the past.
Indeed, circumstances of LDCs differ so much, that there is no point in
formalising generally applicable strategies. However, the questions which
have to be addressed in designing an industrialisation strategy are reasonably clear. Will it generate a set of industries likely to remain viable in terms
of their links with the international economy? Will it accelerate the domestic
accumulation of skill and capital? And will it be compatible with political
structures which are not too repressive?

NOTES

1. In Hans Singer's early deliberations [*1950*], both arguments for industrialisation are present: the uneven distribution of gains in foreign trade and the dynamic internal impulses radiating from industrialisation.
2. In fact, most of the arguments which were so skilfully put together by Little, Scitovsky and Scott in their policy-oriented study, had previously been made by other authors.
3. Compare White's article in this volume which offers both important analytical categories for examining the role of the state and lessons from three waves of socialist industrialisation.
4. Using effective protection rates as efficiency indicators is not without conceptual and empirical problems. The justification is merely pragmatic: first, rates of protection are available for many countries and reasonably comparable; second, the objective is merely one of giving orders of magnitude of the extent to which value added in LDCs diverge from that in the world market. It should be pointed out, however, that the primary objective of those developing the concept of effective protection was to point to the bias in the price system's signals with respect to resource allocation and not to formulate an inefficiency measure.
5. Senghaas [*1977, 1978*] who emphasises the pertinence of List's work to present-day development problems, interprets List in the latter way and argues for temporary but complete (and not selective) dissociation from the world economy; the costs incurred in the process are achnowledged, but considered inevitable for the construction of a viable economy. In contrast, Westphal [*1981*] argues that there is an empirical case for infant industry protection on a selective basis only.
6. On the basis of its recent research, UNCTAD [*1982*] divides LDCs into three groups according to the level of development achieved in the production of capital goods. The most developed group comprises seven countries (China, Brazil, India, the Republic of Korea, Mexico, Singapore and Yugoslavia) whose capital goods sector not only produces a wide range of standard equipment but has also begun to manufacture technologically complex equipment. An intermediate group includes a dozen or so countries in which the production of standard capital equipment is on its way. The third group contains the great majority of LDCs whose capital goods sector is still in an embryonic state. The unevenness is highlighted by the fact that the countries included in the first group account for more than 85 per cent of the total capital goods output of LDCs as a whole.
7. Some studies include India and countries of Southern Europe as well. The widest accounts cover also Malaysia, the Philippines and Indonesia.
8. Based on IBRD, *World Tables*, second edition, 1980. I am grateful to Parvin Alizadeh for working out the statistics used in this paragraph.
9. Calculated from UNCTAD, Handbook of *International Trade and Development Statistics*, 1981 supplement, TD/STAT/10, Geneva, 1982; and from Little, Scitovsky and Scott [*1970: Appendix to Chapter 7*] and Park [*1981*].
10. Based on ILO, *Yearbook of Labour Statistics*, 1973 and 1982.
11. Havrylyshyn and Alikhani [*1982a*] point out that, between 1970 and 1979, a dozen LDCs were able to achieve an increase in exports at rates comparable to the NICs, without however attaining equally high GDP growth.
12. In this context it is worth referring also to the experience of the Republic of Ireland as a case study of late industrialisation under outward-looking policies. O'Malley [*1983*] shows that the apparently successful growth of industry was due largely to Ireland's success in attracting a greatly disproportionate share of the globally limited amount of mobile, export-oriented foreign industrial investment. The country's indigenous or domestically based industries, on the other hand, remained mostly confined to the limited range of activities which had relatively low barriers to entry for newcomers; in fact they showed signs of relative decline.
13. It is perhaps worth noting that these growth rates are in nominal prices; the real rise in volume was lower, but still at an historically impressive rate.
14. The term 'Eurodollar' is not very accurate. The market is neither limited to Europe, nor does it deal only in dollars. A term such as 'transnational currency market' would be more precise.

15. Leudde-Neurath [1983] suggests that existing studies exaggerate the extent of import-liberalisation during the 1960s, since they are either based on a superficial analysis of that period or on a conceptually and empirically flawed micro-analysis of Korea's import controls.
16. In general very little time elapsed between the introduction of export promotion measures and the fulfilment of expectations. (In fact, in the Korean case exports began to grow substantially even before policies were changed.) It is somewhat surprising that few observers have paused to ask why the policies appeared to work almost instantly. It seems that as a result of the extended post-war boom in the world economy, sensitivity to the importance of business cycles somewhat disappeared.
17. They are certainly unlikely to relinquish already conquered markets and make room for other LDCs as assumed in the optimistic visions of Balassa [1981] and others.
18. For an elaboration of this thesis with respect to Kenya, see Kaplinsky [1982].
19. Sutcliffe's paper in this volume further complements this critical assessment of socialist industrialisation, in particular where it is modelled on the Soviet experience. He insists that human suffering and violent political repression in socialist or capitalist countries cannot be justified with an argument that fast industrialisation creates future welfare.

REFERENCES

Albert, B. and P. Hendersen, 1981, 'Latin America and the Great War: A Preliminary Survey of Developments in Chile, Peru, Argentina and Brazil', *World Development*, Vol. 9, No. 8.
Baer, W., 1965, *Industrialization and Economic Development in Brazil*, Homewood Ill.: Richard Irwin.
——, 1972, 'Import Substitution and Industrialization in Latin America: Experiences and Interpretations', *Latin American Research Review* (Spring).
Balassa, B., 1978, 'Export Incentives and Export Performance in Developing Countries: A Comparative Analysis', *Weltwirtschaftliches Archiv*, Band 114, Heft 1.
——, 1981, *The Newly Industrialising Countries in the World Economy*, Oxford: Pergamon Press.
Balassa, B. and Associates, 1971, *The Structure of Protection in Developing Countries*, Baltimore: John Hopkins Press.
Ballance, R., J. Ansari, H. Singer, 1982, *The International Economy and Industrial Development: Trade and Investment in the Third World*, Brighton: Wheatsheaf Books.
Bell, R.M. 1982, 'Technical Change in Infant Industries: A Review of the Empirical Evidence', Science Policy Research Unit, University of Sussex, mimeo.
Bhagwati, J.N., 1978, *Foreign Trade Regimes and Economic Development: Anatomy and Consequences of Exchange Control Regimes*, Cambridge, Mass.: Ballinger Press.
Bienefeld, M.A., 1982a, 'The International Context for National Development Strategies: Constraints and Opportunities in a Changing World', in M.A. Bienefeld and M. Godfrey (eds.), *The Struggle for Development: National Strategies in an International Context*, Chichester: John Wiley.
——, 1982b, 'International Constraints and Opportunities', paper presented to Workshop on Facilitating Indigenous Technological Capability, University of Edinburgh, May 1982.
——, 1982c, 'Tanzanian Industry and Basic Needs: Short and Long Term Issues', Institute of Development Studies, University of Brighton, mimeo.
——, 1982c, 'Tanzanian Industry and Basic Needs: Short and Long Term Issues', Institute of Development Studies, University of Sussex, mimeo.
Bienefeld, M., M. Godfrey, H. Schmitz, 1977, 'Trade Unions and the "New" Internationalization of Production', *Development and Change*, Vol. 8, No. 4, October.
Bruton, H.J., 1970, 'The Import Substitution Strategy of Economic Development: A Survey', *Pakistan Development Review*, Vol. 10, No. 2, reprinted in I. Livingstone, *Development Economics and Policy – Readings*, London: George Allen and Unwin, 1981.
Cardoso, F.H., and E. Faletto, 1970, *Dependência e Desenvolvimento na América Latina*, Rio de Janeiro: Zahar.
Cline, W.R., 1982, 'Can the East Asian Model of Development be Generalised', *World Development*, Vol. 10, No. 2.

Cooper, C., 1980, 'Policy Interventions for Technological Innovation in Developing Countries', *World Bank Staff Working Paper No. 441*, Washington DC.

Cooper, C. and K. Hoffman, 1981, 'Transactions in technology and implications for developing countries', Science Policy Research Unit, University of Sussex, mimeo.

Corden, W.M., 1971, *The Theory of Protection*, Oxford: Clarendon Press.

Dahlman, C., and L. Westphal, 1982, 'Technological effort in industrial development – an interpretative survey of recent research', in F. Stewart and J. James, (eds.) [*1982*].

Datta-Chauduri, M.K., 1981, 'Industrialisation and Foreign Trade: The Development Experiences of South Korea and the Philippines', in E. Lee (ed.) [*1981*].

Dean, W., 1969, *The Industrialization of São Paulo, 1880–1945*, Austin: University of Texas Press.

Dell, S. and R. Lawrence, 1980, *The Balance of Payments Adjustment Process in Developing Countries*, New York: Pergamon Press in cooperation with United Nations.

Diaz-Alejandro, C., 1975, 'Trade Policies and Economic Development', in Peter Kenen (ed.), *International Trade and Finance: Frontiers for Research*, Cambridge: Cambridge University Press.

Donges, J.B., 1976, 'A Comparative Survey of Industrialization Policies in Fifteen Semi-Industrial Countries', *Weltwirtschaftliches Archiv*, Band 112, Heft 4.

Economic Commission for Latin America, 1950, *The Economic Development of Latin America and its Principal Problems* (by R. Prebisch), New York: United Nations, Department of Economic Affairs.

Erber, F., 1983, 'Technological Dependence and Learning Revisited', mimeo, Instituto de Economia Industrial, Faculdade de Economia e Administração, Universidade Federal do Rio de Janeiro.

Frank, A.G., 1971, *Capitalism and Underdevelopment in Latin America*, Harmondsworth: Penguin.

Fransman, M. and K. King (eds.), forthcoming, *Technological Capability in the Third World*, London: Macmillan.

Fröbel, F., J. Heinrichs, O. Kreye, 1977, *Die Neue Internationale Arbeitsteilung*, Reinbek/Hamburg: Rowohlt Verlag.

Germidis, D. (ed.), 1981, *International Subcontracting – A New Form of Investment*, Paris: Development Centre, OECD.

Griffith-Jones, S., 1980, 'The growth of multinational banking, the Euro-currency market and the effects on developing countries', *Journal of Development Studies*, Vol. 16, No. 2, June.

——, 1982, 'Transnational Finance and Latin American National Development', *IDS Discussion Paper No. 175*, University of Sussex.

Hamilton, C., 1983, 'Capitalist Industrialisation in the Four Little Tigers of East Asia', in P. Limqueco and B. McFarlane (eds.), *Neo-Marxist Theories of Development*, London: Croom Helm.

Havrylyshyn, O. and I. Alikhani, 1982a, 'Is There Cause for Export Optimism? An Inquiry into the Existence of a Second Generation of Successful Exporters', *Weltwirtschaftliches Archiv*, Band 118, Heft 4.

——, 1982b, 'Protection Levels and Policies in Developing and Industrial Countries: Annotated Bibliography and Data Bank Summary', International Trade Division, Economic Analysis and Projection Department, The World Bank, mimeo.

Helleiner, G.K., 1981, *Intra-firm trade and the developing countries*, London and Basingstoke: Macmillan.

Hirschman, A.O., 1968, 'The Political Economy of Import Substituting Industrialization in Latin America', *Quarterly Journal of Economics*, Vol. 82, No. 1, February.

Ingham, B. and C. Simmons, 1981, 'The Two World Wars and Economic Development: Editors' Introduction', Special Issue, *World Development*, Vol. 9, No. 8, August.

Joekes, S., 1982, 'Female-led Industrialisation – Women's jobs in Third World Export Manufacturing: The Case of the Moroccan Clothing Industry', *IDS Research Report* No. 15, University of Sussex.

Kaplinsky, R., 1982, 'Fractions of Capital and Accumulation in Kenya', Institute of Development Studies, University of Sussex, mimeo.

Krueger, A.O., 1978, *Foreign Trade Regimes and Economic Development: Liberalization Attempts and Consequences*, Cambridge, Mass.: Ballinger Press.

Krueger, A.O., 1981, 'Export-Led Industrial Growth Reconsidered', in W. Hong and L.B. Krause (eds.), *Trade and Growth of the Advanced Developed Countries in the Pacific Basin*, Seoul: Korea Development Institute.

Lall, S., 1980, 'Exports of Manufactures by Newly Industrializing Countries: A Survey of Recent Trends', *Economic and Political Weekly*, 6 and 13 December.

——, 1982, 'Technological Learning in the Third World: Some Implications of Technology Exports', in F. Stewart and J. James (eds.) [*1982*].

Lee, E., 1981, 'Export-led Industrialisation in Asia: An Overview' in E. Lee (ed.), *Export-led industrialisation and development*, Geneva: Asian Employment Programme, International Labour Office.

List, F., 1841, *Das Nationale System der Politischen Ökonomie*, 1st edition; in English: *The National System of Political Economy*, London: Longmans, Green and Co., 1885.

Little, I.M.D., 1981, 'The Experience and Causes of Rapid Labour-Intensive Development in Korea, Taiwan Province, Hong Kong and Singapore and the Possibilities of Emulation', in E. Lee (ed.) [*1981*].

Little, I., T. Scitovsky, M. Scott, 1970, *Industry and Trade in Some Developing Countries – A Comparative Study*, London, New York, Toronto: Oxford University Press for OECD.

Luedde-Neurath, R., 1983, 'Import Controls and Export Oriented Development: A Re-examination of the South Korean Case 1962–82', Institute of Development Studies, University of Sussex, mimeo.

Malan, P. and R. Bonelli, 1977, 'The Brazilian Economy in the Seventies: Old and New Developments', *World Development*, Vol. 5, Nos. 1/2.

Merhav, M., 1969, *Technological Dependence, Monopoly and Growth*, Oxford: Pergamon Press.

Miller, R., 1981, 'Latin American Manufacturing and the First World War: An Exploratory Essay', *World Development*, Vol. 9, No. 8, August.

Nayyar, D., 1978, 'Transnational Corporations and Manufactured Exports from Poor Countries', *The Economic Journal*, Vol. 88, March.

Nixson, F., 1982, 'Import-Substituting Industrialization' in M. Fransman (ed.), *Industry and Accumulation in Africa*, London: Heinemann.

North American Congress on Latin America (NACLA), 1975, 'Hit and Run, US Runaway Shops on the Mexican Border', *NACLA Report*, Vol. IX, No. 5, July-August.

O'Malley, E., 1983, 'Late Industrialisation under Outward-Looking Policies: The Experience and Prospects of the Republic of Ireland', D. Phil. thesis, University of Sussex.

Pack, H., 1981, 'Fostering the Capital-Goods Sector in LDCs', *World Development*, Vol. 9, No. 3, March.

Park, N.C., 1981, 'Export-led Industrialisation: The Korean Experience 1960–1978', in E. Lee (ed.) [*1981*].

Prebisch, R., 1959, 'Commercial Policy in the Underdeveloped Countries', *American Economic Review*, Papers and Proceedings, Vol. 49, May.

——, 1964, 'Towards a New Trade Policy for Development', in *Proceedings of the United Nations Conference on Trade and Development*, Vol. II, United Nations, New York.

Ranis, G., 1981, 'Challenges and Opportunities Posed by Asia's Super Exporters: Implications for Manufactured Exports from Latin America', in W. Baer and M. Gillis, *Export Diversification and the New Protectionism – The Experiences of Latin America*, National Bureau of Economic Research and the Bureau of Economic and Business Research, University of Illinois.

Rosenberg, N., 1976, *Perspectives on Technology*, Cambridge: Cambridge University Press.

Schmitz, H., 1982, *Manufacturing in the Backyard – Case Studies on Accumulation and Employment in Small-scale Brazilian Industry*, London: Frances Pinter.

Senghaas, D., 1977, 'Friedrich List and the New International Economic Order', *Economics*, Vol. 15.

——, 1978, 'Dissociation and Autocentric Development, An Alternative Development Policy for the Third World', *Economics*, Vol. 18.

Singer, H.W., 1950, 'The Distribution of Gains Between Investing and Borrowing Countries', *American Economic Review*, Papers and Proceedings, Vol. XL, May.

Singh, A., 1983, 'Third World Industrialisation: Industrial Strategies and Policies in the 1980s and 1990s'. (Paper prepared for the High-Level Expert Group Meeting on Industrial

Development Strategies and Policies for Developing Countries, organised by UNIDO and the Government of Peru), mimeo, Faculty of Economics, University of Cambridge, April.

Spiegel, L., 1980, 'Delicate Bonds: The Global Semiconductor Industry', *Pacific Research*, Vol. 11, No. 1.

Stewart, F., 1976, 'Capital Goods in Developing Countries', in A. Cairncross and M. Puri (eds.), *Employment, Income Distribution and Development Strategy: Problems of the Developing Countries: Essays in Honour of Hans Singer*, London: Macmillan.

Stewart, F., and J. James, (eds.), 1982, *The Economics of New Technology in Developing Countries*, London: Frances Pinter.

Sunkel, O., 1973, 'Transnational Capitalism and National Disintegration in Latin America', *Social and Economic Studies*, Vol. 22, No. 1, March.

Sutcliffe, R.B., 1971, *Industry and Underdevelopment*, London: Addison-Wesley.

Tavares, M.C., 1964, 'The Growth and Decline of Import Substitution in Brazil', ECLA, *Economic Bulletin for Latin America*, Vol. IX, No. 1, March, New York: United Nations.

Thomas, C.Y., 1974, *Dependence and Transformation*, New York: Monthly Review Press.

Tyler, W.G., 1976, *Manufactured Export Expansion and Industrialisation in Brazil*, Tübingen: J.C.B. Mohr.

UNCTAD, 1982, *The Capital Goods and Industrial Machinery Sector in Developing Countries: Issues in the Transfer and Development of Technology*, TD/B/C6/AC7/2, Geneva, May.

Vaitsos, C.V., 1974, *Intercountry Income Distribution and Transnational Enterprises*, Oxford: Oxford University Press.

——, 1978, 'Crisis in Regional Economic Cooperation (Integration) Among Developing Countries: A Survey', *World Development*, Vol. 6, No. 6, June.

Villela, A.V. and W. Suzigan, 1977, 'Government Policy and the Economic Growth of Brazil, 1889–1945', IPEA, *Brazilian Economic Studies*, No. 3, Rio de Janeiro.

Wade, R., 1982, *Irrigation and Agricultural Politics in South Korea*, Boulder, Colorado: Westview Press.

Westphal, L., 1978, 'The Republic of Korea's Experience with Export-led Industrial Development', *World Development*, Vol. 6, No. 3, March.

——, 1981, 'Empirical Justification for Infant Industry Protection', *World Bank Staff Working Paper* 445, Washington, D.C.

Trade, Industrialisation, and the Visible Hand

by David Evans and Parvin Alizadeh*

The paper examines the neo-classical case for the export-orientated industrialisation strategy, questioning not only its representation of what has occurred in the Newly Industrialising Countries, but also raising some doubts about the validity of the analytical model which is implicit in its policy prescriptions. An alternative analytical framework and political economy model is then sketched out. The experience of South Korea and Taiwan is used for illustrative purposes, highlighting areas where further conceptual and empirical analysis is required to give a fully-blown alternative story. An appendix offers a brief summary and critique of some recent neo-classical work on the relationship between price distortion and growth.

This paper presents a brief critique of the neo-classical case for the export-orientated industrialisation (EOI) strategy, questioning not only its representation of what has occurred in the Newly Industrialising Countries (NICs), but also raising some doubts about the validity of the analytical model which is implicit in its policy prescriptions. We then sketch out an alternative analytical framework and political economy model which we believe provides a sounder basis on which the NIC experience can be assessed, highlighting areas where further conceptual and empirical analysis is required to give a fully-blown alternative story.

SUMMARY OF THE NEO-CLASSICAL CASE FOR EOI

In the context of neo-classical and world orthodoxy, the Ranis interpretation of the EOI strategy [*Ranis 1981*] provides probably the clearest analytical account. We present a brief summary of some of the salient points, with some supplementation from other neo-classical authors, not with the intention of setting up a straw-man, but in order to help explore the limits of the

* Institute of Development Studies at the University of Sussex. We are grateful to the participants in the IDS Industrialisation cluster, the participants of the SSRC Development Economics Working Group Conference on Trade and Development held at the University of Warwick in May 1983, and the participants of the Journal of Contemporary Asia Conference on Industrialisation and the Labour Process in S.E. Asia held in Copenhagen, August 1983, for providing a forum for discussion and comment on earlier drafts of this paper. We are particularly grateful to Raphie Kaplinsky as editor of the series and to Melanie Beresford, Mike Cowen, Clive Hamilton, Chris Gregory, Colin Kirkpatrick, Richard Luedde-Neurath, Jerzy Osiatynski, Gus Ranis, Hubert Schmitz, John Sender, Alasdair Smith, Robert Wade and Gordon White. We thank them all but implicate none.

neo-classical analysis.[1] Ranis takes the East Asian NICs, South Korea and Taiwan, as the paradigm cases, excluding Hong Kong and Singapore as special city-state cases without wider applicability. South Korea and Taiwan are distinguished from other LDCs and notably other Latin America NICs by two main criteria:

(a) Although in the early 1950s these countries pursued an import-substituting industrialisation (ISI) strategy via the usual policy package of tariffs, import licensing, low interest rates, and so on, they nevertheless chose a milder version of the strategy than is typically the case. This meant that the undesirable consequences of ISI were less pronounced than in other LDCs, reflected in a relatively lower effective rate of protection, lower capital intensity in production and less unfavourable policies towards agriculture. During this phase of labour-intensive industrial growth or Primary Import Substitution (PIS), non-durable consumer goods production for the domestic market was expanded rapidly. Industrial growth in this phase was accompanied in part by the export of land- or resource-based primary products, which helped provide non-competing import requirements for PIS, supplemented by aid and foreign capital. Ranis argues that Taiwan relied rather less than South Korea on aid and foreign capital, reflecting the different relative endowment of land and natural resources in the two countries. This process of PIS lasted until the end of the 1950s and the beginning of the 1960s, when the supply of foreign exchange and the size of the domestic market became a constraint on growth.

(b) On completion of the PIS phase, South Korea and Taiwan moved towards exports of the same labour-intensive non-durable consumer goods in the Primary Export Substitution phase (PES). This is contrasted with many other LDCs that moved directly from PIS into production of durable consumer goods, intermediate and capital goods – all capital, skill and technology intensive products in comparison with those favoured under PIS and PES. This in turn implied prolonging ISI policies or the development of subsidised export promotion, the maintenance and possible increase in the levels of protection and continued neglect of agriculture. In contrast, the PES strategy was accompanied by a shift in public policy towards lower protection on product and capital markets, exchange rate reform, and so on, the familiar elements of the open-economy market-orientated EOI strategy.

Broadly speaking, protection in the initial PIS phase of industrialisation is justified by some combination of the infant industry, external economic and economies of scale arguments.[2] The amount of effective protection justified in practice by such arguments varies between different neo-classical writers, but most would argue for maximum protection of 10 per cent to 20 per cent with an infant industry learning period of five to eight years. The underlying reason for the shift towards PES in the neo-classical story is the gradual shift from comparative advantage premised on land/resources or aid and foreign capital to comparative advantage based on unskilled labour. Given the higher initial relative endowment of resources in Taiwan, compared with South Korea,[3] the transition to a more open trading regime based on unskilled labour was more urgent in the latter case. In contrast, in the case of the Philippines and several Latin American countries examined, the relative abundance of resources permitted the bypassing of the PES phase and the possibility that EOI would degenerate to export promotion at any cost. The shift of the East Asian NICs towards PES absorbed much unskilled labour, given the relatively unlimited opportunities for growth in the world market. This, in turn, led to more equitable income distribution as employment opportunities expanded rapidly, and a more robust and flexible development process as further import and export substitution took place in more capital- and skill-intensive commodities. PES as the first step in an EOI strategy is sharply contrasted with export promotion *without* such a clear-cut reference to comparative advantage. Thus it is argued, the advantages of lower capital/output ratios, fewer demanding 'infant industries' which refuse to grow up, and the stimulus of greater competitiveness from a world-market orientation, give the paradigm East Asia NICs a decisive edge in terms of growth rates and capacity to adjust to the shocks of the world market. There is a strong caution against prolonging the ISI phase into capital and durable consumer goods industries, so that a switch towards EOI exposes the danger of export promotion regardless of underlying comparative advantages.

SOME ANALYTICAL ISSUES

In the neo-classical story, the principal social process through which 'development' is achieved is the extension and perfection of market relations. For example, the 1983 World Development Report [*World Bank, 1983: Ch. 6*] sketches the theoretical case behind this proposition and offers a new contribution to the empirical evidence, summarised in the Appendix of this paper, of the association between price distortion and low rates of growth.

The positive economic theory behind the neo-classical analysis of the trade and development story of the NICs is the modern factor proportions theory of comparative advantage. In the simplest case, this is based upon a single-country Heckscher–Ohlin–Samuelson (H–O–S) trade model, modified to allow for an institutional wage in the early stages of rapid accumulation governed by surplus labour in agriculture [*Caves and Jones: 1981, Ch. 6-8; Fei and Ranis, 1964; Krueger, 1977*]. The wider implications of the NIC strategy can also be analysed in terms of a two-country, north–south or core–periphery version of the H–O–S model appropriately specified. The neo-classical trade policy for the NICs draws on the findings of modern neo-classical welfare economics, especially the theory of the second-best, applied to international trade issues [*Corden, 1974*]. At a technical level, this analytical framework can be elaborated in many ways. In the hands of neo-classical economists, it has been applied in both positive and normative analyses of the trade and development aspects of the NIC experience in a breathtaking array of countries and historical experiences. It is therefore important to examine the assumptions often made by neo-classical economists in deploying such a model.

(1) There are a range of issues which arise from the way in which the neo-classical approach abstracts the economic from the social and political dimension of the analysis. These arise from the *prescriptive* rather than *descriptive* nature of neo-classical economic analysis.[4] The neo-classical approach tends to abstract from the social determination of the technical coefficients, or parameters governing behavioural relationships in production and consumption. Class relationships are usually defined at the level of the market by the functional distribution of income, with no reference to class relationships at the point of production. If class relationships and class struggle are an important part of the specification of the social and political dimension of the economic analysis, so are they important in the conceptualisation of the form and character of the state.

A characteristic of all late development has been the pervasive involvement of an interventionist state [*Gershenkron, 1966*]. A recent survey of the role of the state in development argues that an analysis of the effectiveness of the developmental state must rest on three basic factors: its social nature, its political–administrative capacity and the specific modes of involvement (White, in this volume). There is a strong correlation between neo-classical economic analysis and a conceptualisation of a liberal, or in its strong version used by Ranis, a catalytic state acting in the public interest [*Ranis, 1981*]. Such analyses tend to conflate these three distinct dimensions of the developmental state into arguments over parametric versus pervasive forms of involvement of the state. The former implies a certain degree of autonomy of economic agents with state intervention confined to the provision of a regulative framework and infrastructural capacity, whilst the latter involves direct or mediated organisational penetration by the state at every level and a circumscribed autonomy of economic agents. The neo-classical benchmark against which such intervention is to be assessed is the free-market outcome, appropriately adjusted via arm's-length taxes, subsidies and lump-sum redistribution to take into account all forms of imperfection and deviation of social from private cost and benefit. Not surprisingly, parametric intervention is seen in a favourable light in these forms of analysis and the pervasive forms of intervention are usually either 'inefficient' or not seen at all.[5] We will return to these issues later; for present purposes the analytical point to note is the importance of carrying within the conceptualisation of the economic, even at a high level of abstraction, a strong notion of the inherently social and political character of these relationships.

It is not enough to discuss the role of the developmental state in the rise of market relationships, both at the level of circulation and production, without adding a territorial dimension. Just as capitalism requires a state to perform a wide range of economic functions to ensure its reproduction, so it requires the state to define its territorial limits and to mediate its relations with the world economy [*Murray, 1975: 108-28*]. The history of trade and the rise of exchange relationships can be thought of as the rise of the division of labour between town and country. The development of the forces of production might be characterised as an historical process by which activities formerly carried out in the country (for example, handicrafts and domestic industry of all kinds produced under peasant, feudal or whatever form of pre-capitalist relations) are increasingly produced in towns (either in factories or under conditions which attempt to bring the factory to the mine or farm).[6] More abstractly, Bukharin [*1972: 25-6*] put it most succinctly when he conceptualised the world economy as a system of production relations and, correspondingly, a set of exchange relations on a world scale. Thus our simple town–country division can be expanded to conceptualise a simultaneous process of internationalisation of the relations of production and exchange, and a process of nationalisation and the rise of the modern nation state. Regional and *foreign* trade is transformed into regional and *international* trade, with some nations becoming gigantic factories – the industrialised centre of the world economy – and others becoming agrarian or semi-agrarian colonies, states or regions. It is within this context that the NICs have emerged as strong independent industrialised nation states from their historically determined agrarian and colonial position in the international division of labour.

These considerations have strong implications for the discussion of the theory of comparative advantage, upon which much of the neo-classical analysis of the trade and growth aspects of the NIC phenomenom is based. Several neo-classical writers have attempted to deal with some of these issues in their abstract conceptualisation of regional and international trade and the notion of comparative advantage [*Williams, 1929*], [*Ohlin, 1932*] and [*Kindleberger, 1962*], and the Ranis perspectives tend to flow from this tradition. Other modern-day followers of the neo-classical tradition – represented here in the analyses of the NICs – have not been so careful. They have tended to reduce questions of trade and industrialisation policy to the purely economic analysis of given comparative advantage and the rational choice of policy-makers acting in the public interest, a good example being Little [*1981: 25*], who ascribes the NIC experience as being 'almost entirely due to good policies and the ability of the people'. The notion of comparative advantage, its determinants, and the position of policy-makers acting to develop, enhance and change the pattern of comparative advantage is surely more complex. In down-playing the social, political and historical dimensions of the concept of comparative advantage, error is invited in both the attribution of causality of comparative advantage and in more narrowly prescribing the limits within which developmental choices can be made.

What is the relevance of all this for the neo-classical analysis of EOI? At the most general level, the neo-classical approach abstracts from the historical specificity of the East Asian NIC model. In other words, there is a mis-specification or an incomplete specification of the internal and external economic, social and political conditions which underwrite the success of the East Asian model. This has implications both for the reproducibility of the model and the choice of policy instruments. White [*1984, in this volume*] distinguishes between the three most prevalent forms of the development state, not on the basis of more or less market, but on the basis of the class character of the state and different patterns of pervasive intervention. Thus, he distinguishes: (i) state capitalist countries in which the state and private capital are closely interlocked with a set of pervasive controls on economic agents; (ii) intermediate regimes [*Kalecki, 1967*] in which industrial capital is severely circumscribed by a massive expansion of state ownership and management with a state-class emerging to dominate civil society; (iii) state socialist regimes where private industrial capital is largely eliminated and where the revolutionary coalition builds a state with all-penetrating multi-faceted pervasive controls. Within this taxonomy, the East Asian NICs are clearly state capitalist. In so far as they are a paradigm case for neo-classical analysts, appraisal should therefore be confined to an assessment of state capitalist NICs. Whilst we should not expect the model to perform well outside its chosen terrain, there are also powerful arguments for suggesting an important element of historical specificity for different social formations within the broadly defined state capitalist category.

How was it that particular forms of state and class relationships arose leading to successful state capitalism in the East Asian NICs? Hamilton provides a sketch of how this happened for the case of the 'four little tigers' – Singapore, Hong Kong, South Korea and Taiwan, and how each case fitted into the world economy and the international division of labour [*Hamilton, 1983*]. Of crucial importance in Hamilton's discussion is the development of industrial capitalism in South Korea and Taiwan through the colonial period to a privileged relationship with the US in the present geo-political arrangements. In the process of class formation in both South Korea and Taiwan in the 1950s and early 1960s, industrial capital, in alliance with state strata such as the military, the bureaucracy and (in Taiwan) the party elite, triumphed over landed interests and merchant capital in the struggle for dominance. Collectively, capitalist classes establish their dominance over labour – whether peasant or the growing wage-labour force – during the same period. This approach helps to build an understanding of the internal social character and basis of the state in these cases. It attempts an account of the relationship between social and political forces and the accidents of history in the determination of the initial resource endowments. The interaction between these developing class relationships, the nature of political conflict in the region which produced the emigrations of skilled professional classes, and the cultural factors leading to a stress on education, all contributed to the development of a strong political and administrative capacity in the emerging South Korean and Taiwanese states. These favourable elements, which permit the reproduction of industrial capitalism, combined with a set of parametric and pervasive forms of state intervention in all branches of the economy (examined in more detail below) to allow the state to emerge as a strategic centre in the development process. The state mediated internal and external relations, planned investment and technological advance, guided industrial structure changes and so on, enabling these countries to industrialise so successfully through a brief ISI phase to the EOI model from the beginning of the 1960s.

In summary, we might characterise the set of macro- and micro-class relationships and forms of pervasive state intervention described above as the Social Structure of Accumulation (SSA), to borrow a phrase coined in the analysis of the economic, social and political determinants of post-war profitability in the US economy [*Bowles et al., 1983*]. Inherently, the forms of pervasive state intervention which underline the NIC success stories imply a set of policy instruments which lie outside the range of neo-classical policy analyses since they usually require forms of direct intervention which rely on highly specific social structures and social relations for their success. Since such social structures tend to be specific to a particular social formation, they may not be amenable to transformation into parametric forms of intervention which are more easily reproducible in other social formations. Fundamentally, the neo-classical analysis of the NICs fails to take into account the SSA. This proposition is further explored in the Appendix, which offers a critique of recent World Bank work on the relationship between price distortions and low growth and the role of institutional and other explanations in 'explaining' what is unexplained by the price distortion–growth relationship.

(2) The remarks above suggest that the full range of policy instruments, especially the pervasive forms of state intervention, are seldom examined by neo-classical economists in the normative or policy analysis. Here, we focus on the positive side of the models. The way in which the models work is important for understanding the underlying causes of comparative advantage and growth. Indirectly, this understanding of how the real economy works is important in the analysis of policy. The simplest point of entry to the issues which divide most economists between neo-classical and more classical approaches is through the theory of profit. (A more extended summary discussion of some of the issues which underline this section can be found in [*Walsh and Gram, 1980: Ch. 16*].) Neo-classical approaches apply some form of the marginal principle in the determination of profit to the portrayal of an abstract capitalist economy. Classical approaches apply some form of the surplus principle whereby either wages or profits are determined by some other mechanism exogenous to the economic model and the returns to the other 'factor' are given by the remaining surplus. This has important implications for the theory of comparative advantage. In traditional H–O–S trade theory, aggregate capital is important both as a determinant of comparative advantage. In this view, other things being equal, the relative endowment of the 'factors' labour, capital and/or land determine the pattern of trade and the shifts in 'factor' prices accompanying either the opening of trade or a change in the trading regime. General equilibrium theorists would agree that there are analytical issues arising from the capital theory debates of the 1960s which cannot be safely ignored, not least for models of trade in which endowments of capital are a determinant of comparative advantage [*Samuelson, 1975; Ethier, 1979; Smith, 1984*].

Within a fully specified inter-temporal general equilibrium model with produced means of production there is no problem of homogeneous versus heterogeneous capital. The valuation of the stock of heterogeneous capital is just a question of adding up the individual components of aggregate capital at the appropriate prices. What does matter (at this level of abstraction) is the concept of equilibrium in the definition of aggregate capital. This in turn has implications for the role of aggregate capital as a determinant of comparative advantage and the conceptualisation of dynamic adjustment through time. Here, the debates over neo-Ricardian or Sraffian trade theory are important [*Ethier, 1979; Metcalfe and Steedman, 1981; Smith, 1984*]. Put most simply, many propositions which are taken as self-evident in the neo-classical discussion of the NICs, can not be taken for granted. For example, the observation which derives from static H–O–S theory that an abundant endowment of labour relative to capital is the *cause* (*ceteris paribus*) of relatively low wages, leading to a comparative advantage in labour-intensive commodities, with favourable income distribution consequences for export-led growth, no longer holds. In the more complex heterogeneous capital world, one can only *describe* the characteristics of a trading equilibrium as being associated with the export of labour or capital-intensive commodities (in the two-factor case). Thus, even at the most abstract level, the question of what *causes* comparative advantage is qualified in an important way.

The natural long-run dynamic extension of the H–O–S model is based on a non-steady state growth model in which savings and investment are endogenous. In addition to the usual set of strong or 'incredible' assumptions about behaviour which characterises the static general equilibrium model, such as perfect competition, utility maximisation as the sole choice criteria in consumption, profit maximisation in production, and no externalities in consumption or production, it must be assumed that at any given point in time there is a complete set of markets for all commodities at every future point in time. The resulting bench-mark optimal inter-temporal growth path becomes the central focus for the analysis of trade and welfare [*Smith, 1984*]. The initial endowments of the three main sets of productive 'factors': labour, land/resources and heterogeneous capital or machines play an important role in describing comparative advantage only in the short and medium run. In the long run the endogenous savings behaviour and population growth will govern the supply of finance capital (produced means of production valued at an appropriate set of prices) relative to the supply of labour and land, and comparative advantage will be determined by these new behavioural relationships.

The central problem with this line of reasoning is not the use of incredible assumptions for analytical models. Rather, for any capitalist economy in which the incredible assumptions are necessarily violated, it is important which strategic assumptions are made in order to insert greater descriptive reality into the model. Here, three interrelated sets of strategic assumptions of neo-Ricardian trade theory seem useful for the analysis of trade and development in the NICs:

(i) concentrating on some form of the surplus principle for the determination of distribution, a simple framework is provided for the analysis of the economic consequences of a wide range of conflictive and non-conflictive behaviour in the market and at the point of production in the accumulation process. No pretence is made that those underlying social processes can be reduced to the economic calculus of a formal model.

(ii) the approach uses a comparative dynamic analysis [*Steedman, 1979b: Ch. 2*] based on a comparison of alternative steady/state growth paths which exist at any point in time, retaining most of the assumptions of the dynamic H–O–S model except full employment and the relationship between inter-temporal time preference and the rate of interest (profit). Rather than attempting any general bench-mark analysis of the dynamic growth path, it seems more useful for many purposes to rely on general qualitative assess-ment of any real historical development trajectory. For example, Mainwar-ing [*1979b*] uses a simple example of disequilibrium in a transition from autarky to trade to make some general observations on the character of dynamic adjustment under capitalism, rather than to look at such a path as a deviation from a more perfect bench-mark norm.

(iii) the combination of the surplus principle and the absence of general assumptions about the level of activity and market clearance on the compa-rative dynamic growth path means that income distribution itself becomes one of the central determinants of comparative advantage.

One way of illuminating these issues is to look at export-led growth in a single-country neo-Ricardian trade model. In the initial ISI phase, land- or resource-based products initially dominate domestic production and exports, with manufactured goods dominating imports. Such a country would be a price taker on the world market, so that with real wages deter-mined by Ricardo–Marx–Lewis cost of labour-power or subsistence wage conditions, the rate of profit will be determined.[7] Given a sufficiently high rate of profit and high enough domestic and foreign savings, rapid growth along Ranis PIS lines can be generated. Similarly, PES can be described with reference to similar wage-profit determination provided surplus-labour con-ditions continue to dominate the long-run wage-determination process. Thus far, there is little disagreement between neo-classical and neo-Ricardian approaches, save the greater emphasis on the disequilibrium character of any actual dynamic path in the latter view. In a similar vein, assessment of transitions to the development of exports of more skill, capital and technology-intensive consumer durables or capital goods raises no analytical issues. Rather, it is the transition from labour-surplus to labour-scarcity conditions which raises a point of analytical interest concerning the determination of profits.

If surplus labour no longer dominates the determination of the wage, what will replace this mechanism to provide the distribution closure in our very simple comparative dynamic model? There are at least three possibilities which have been canvassed in the literature which can be mentioned here. The first would be a continuation of a long-run institutional wage-determination mechanism based on some kind of bargaining model involv-ing the strength of worker organisations together with historical and moral elements, in which the rate of profit is determined as a residual [e.g. *Emmanuel, 1972*]. Second, if national capital is dominant and the wage-profit relation is not subject to competition via international capital flows, some form of Cambridge or Kaleckian determination of the distribution closure from the profit side in which wages are a residual, without reference to inter-temporal time preference would be a possibility [*Metcalfe and Steedman, 1979; Taylor, 1979: Ch. 7; Evans, 1984*]. This approach focuses on the expectations of long-run growth and the savings behaviour and monopoly power of capitalists in determining the rate of profit, variables over which capitalists (and their friends in the state apparatus) have some individual and collective power.[8] Finally, if international capital flows are sufficiently important to bring about a long-run tendency for the equalisation of national and international rates of profit, the rate of profit will be determined by the ruling international rate in the small country case. Thus, in the latter two cases, real wages are determined as residual once world prices and the national or international rate of profit are given. Let us examine these three distribution closures in more detail.

The long-run real wage bargain model which figures so strongly in the Unequal Exchange literature should be ruled out. This account is not very satisfactory since it fails to take fully into account the power of capital to influence the conditions under which capital accumulation takes place. In addition, when there is international capital mobility in the long run, as is assumed in the Unequal Exchange literature, there is nothing in the bargaining theory to prevent capitalists from undermining a real wage which is too high through capital mobility. More helpful for the NIC discussion is the second alternative in which national determinants of the rate of profit along Cambridge or Kaleckian lines. This goes together with the state capitalist character of South Korea and Taiwan as the paradigm NIC cases with the state having a very important direct and indirect effect on the level of profitability and of investment.[9] This is not to say that international profitability is of no importance in determining the role of profit within the NICs; rather, it is argued that the combination of state capitalism and all its controls sufficiently mutes any medium-run tendency for the international determinants to be dominant. It is in the long run that international determinants are likely to be most dominant. Moreover, any extended analysis of the determinants of profit must distinguish between the rate of interest which applies to finance capital and the rate of profit for industrial capital proper, a distinction which is obliterated in the abstract circulating capital model. From the point of view of labour, if the long-run real wage bargain model of factor price determination is ruled out, the rate of profit will be given, whether national of international determinants are dominant. It follows that a very important part of a successful NIC strategy will resolve around the process of getting the price of labour power right, ensuring that the real wage is consistent with given profitability, world prices, and productive techniques. Both analytically and in political economy terms, there are sharp differences between neo-Ricardian and neo-classical accounts as to how this might come about.

In the neo-classical account, it is a built-in tendency towards full employment supply and demand which regulates the market-clearing or equilibrium wage. In the neo-Ricardian world, there is no requirement that the endogenous wage rate be determined by the forces of supply and demand since there is a strong separation between the micro-economic determinants of relative prices (and the pattern of trade) and the macro-economic determinants of employment, the level of activity and the rate of accumulation. Given the presumption of disequilibrium in the process of capital accumulation, this analytical separation readily facilitates a discussion of the political economy mechanism so important in the NICs in making sure that the price of labour power is right. Similarly, this analytical separation between the micro and macro levels of analysis facilitates a discussion of the determinants of comparative advantage without reference to assumptions about market clearance or the endowments of finance capital as in the static H–O–S case. Comparative advantage will be governed by the available set of production techniques, consumer preferences and the determinants of wages or profits. Factor endowments as the *cause* of comparative advantage, so important in the static neo-classical story break down. At best, one can *describe* the relationship between factor intensity of the commodities which enter trade and the relative amounts of finance capital used in alternative comparative dynamic paths. If one is prepared to construct a story about the relative supply of finance capital in relation to population growth, and track the economy through time on the equilibrium non-steady state inter-temporal time path, then the relative supply and demand of finance capital will be a causal determinant of comparative advantage. This very limited view of the forces of supply and demand must be supplemented with an analysis of the political economy determinants of the economic variables and behavioural relationships not explained in the models [*Rowthorn, 1974: 73-4*]. Put in this way, the essential differences between the neo-classical and neo-Ricardian theory of comparative advantage boils down to a debate over the determinants of the rate of profit, the time scale and effectiveness of the long-run forces of supply and demand, and the relative importance of an analysis of the underlying social processes. It is to the political economy issues that we now turn.

THE POLITICAL ECONOMY OF EXPORT-LED GROWTH

Our remarks in this section are intended to be speculative and suggestive, in order to spell out some of the areas in which a development of qualitative political economy arguments seem essential. We also address ourselves briefly to the manner in which the NIC experience in the paradigm Taiwan and especially the South Korea cases is recounted in the neo-classical models under discussion.

We have already illustrated the discussion of the concept of the Social Structure of Accumulation with reference to specific features of the development of the South Korean and Taiwanese states, particularly in the specification of the forms of pervasive intervention of the state and the institutional forms which tend to be reproduced by capital. Returning for a moment to the Ranis discussion of the East Asian NICs, it would appear quite inadequate to characterise the South Korean and Taiwanese states as catalytic, for this tells one little about the specific character of the state in each case and the possibilities for reproducing such favourable conditions in other NICs. For example, Taiwan is a rather unique capitalist economy in which the state apparatus is dominated by a one-party political system and the party itself is run on Leninist principles [*White, in this volume*].

In South Korea the post-colonial bureaucracy which runs the state apparatus remained deeply affected by the Japanese colonial experience with powerful internal checks and balances to control corruption. During the 1960s South Korea developed a strong concensus about national economic development. By combining planning and budgetary functions within a single ministry, the state developed a capacity for taking a strategic role in the formulation and execution of development strategy. Through the development of industry associations, the distinction between the bureaucracy and private business has been blurred. These factors combined with a flexible bureaucratic structure and the decentralisation of non-strategic decision making which permitted cross-subsidisation of exports through the granting of import licenses, to provide a framework whereby internal competitive market processes were powerfully modified without creating an environment for unproductive rent-seeking activity.[10]

Other aspects of the favourable conditions in Taiwan and South Korea underline the difficulties in reproducing the models. We have mentioned above the favourable historical conditions which allowed radical land reform to be carried out in the late 1940s and early 1950s in both Taiwan and South Korea. This prevented the re-establishment of strong landed interests in the countryside and allowed the state to establish strong institutions to foster agricultural development based on a smallholder system [*Wade, 1983a, 1983b*]. Another important but contentious issue is the length of the learning period, and the most desirable PIS period. From much of the neo-classical discussion, it is easy to get the impression that five to eight years is long enough, but both in Taiwan and South Korea PIS industrialisation began in the 1910s and 1920s with an associated long learning period [*Westphal et al., 1981: 8*]. How long, therefore, is the infant industry learning curve, and how much can it be shortened under different historical conditions? (See also Bell [*1983*], and Kaplinsky [*1984b*].) In Korea, for example, the share of the manufacturing sector in net commodity product (in 1936 prices) rose from around 3.5 per cent during 1910–15 to 22 per cent in 1940 [*Westphal et al., 1981: 6*]. This early industrialisation played a key role in laying the foundation for Korea's development of an industrial working class and the beginnings of an industrial capitalist class in spite of Japanese control.[11] Paid employment in manufacturing increased from 23,000 to 4,401,000 between 1910 and 1940, and by 1944 there were 7,000 Korean managers and 28,000 professional and technical workers[12] [*Jones and Sarkong, 1980: 28*]. Moreover, after the Korean War a substantial number of entrepreneurs and professional and technical personnel migrated from the North and concentrated in what is now South Korea. Lastly, it is worth noting that by 1960, there was universal primary education and adult literacy in the South [*Westphal et al., 1981: 10*].

The special nature of South Korea's experience is not confined to the development of its human resources or its depth of industrial reconstruction; foreign aid inflows were significant, reflecting South Korea's geo-strategic position [*Krueger, 1979: Ch.1, 2 and pp.205-12*]. Moreover purchases by the US military were particularly important in stimulating labour-intensive industries which subsequently became significant early exporters in the PES phase [*Westphal et al., 1981: 25*], an important aspect of the more generally favourable world market conditions surrounding the East Asian experience.

The neo-classical discussion of wage policies required for the successful realisation of comparative advantage in the NICs, whether in the surplus-labour or labour scarcity phase, is often presented crudely as a question of eliminating state and institutional intervention inimicable to a market or supply and demand determination of the wage. More careful accounts, for example [*Dhatta-Choudhuri, 1981*], examine the institutional conditions required for the smooth and efficient operation of the labour market. What is usually left out of account in either case is the specific character of the capitalist labour process developed or implanted in the industrialisation process and the tendencies which historically have underlined its development. The pervasive forms of control of labour mobilised by capital and the state, and the relationship of these processes to the operation of the labour market, are of considerable importance. For example, in the Marxian tradition, the transition from formal to real subordination of labour (roughly, the control of labour via the wage contract and the control of labour through the development of machinery and scientific management) as the capitalist labour process develops is emphasised [*Brighton Labour Process Group, 1977; Elbaum, Lazorick, Wilkinson and Zeitlin, 1979; Schmitz, 1983*]. In this context, it is not just technical (in the engineering sense) or choice of technique in the strict economic sense which is important but the interplay between class formation and class struggle at the point of production which conditions and governs the techniques of production chosen, and the dynamic of technical change. Historically, it has been the development of the real subordination of labour which has played a crucial role in enabling capital in the developed capitalist world to retain the upper hand in struggles over developing trade union power.[13] This suggests that it is important to analyse the specific forms of subordination of labour adopted by capital in the development of the NICs, particularly after the end of surplus-labour, and the consequences for the operation of the labour market.[14] Moreover, the NICs have not been able to contain the development of working-class power without the direct intervention of state power. Thus there is no disagreement over the need to get the price of labour power right for successful NIC development. The question which concerns us is the importance of particular social and political determinants, and the crucial visible and pervasive hand of capital and the state, which are such important parts of the story in individual social formations and at particular points of time. This inevitably severely circumscribes the generalisability of any paradigm NIC model to other LDCs.

In our discussion of the relationship between price distortion and growth in the Appendix, shown in Figure 1, we implicitly accepted the weight of World Bank and neo-classical economist's judgement that South Korea is low or even close to a free-trade pricing structure for manufactured goods [*Krueger, 1983: 43 and Table 1; Agarwala, 1983: 20 and Table 5*]. However, the trading regime remained one in which import and export substitution was pursued in a protected environment in which both parametric and pervasive forms of state intervention remained crucial. On the import side this made extensive use of made-to-measure tariffs and quantitative restrictions [*Luedde-Neurath, 1983*]. For example, in 1970, out of 1,312 basic items, the import of 524 were restricted, and 73 were banned altogether [*Sen, 1981: 297; Frank, Kim and Westphal, 1975: 59*]. Since there remains widespread use of quantitative controls, it is argued that South Korea would grow even faster if the form of state intervention shifted to arm's-length intervention through the price mechanism, with tariffs (or even better, subsidies) replacing quantitative controls where continued protection can be justified [*Lal, 1983: 46-7*]. In terms of Figure 1, South Korea can improve its growth through further elimination of price distortions. Our interpretation suggests that this outcome would by no means be assured. If the particular South Korean SSA, combined with EOI, is the key to the success of industrial capitalism in South Korea, then to replace the present SSA in South Korea by arm's-length intervention through the price mechanism may undermine that success. It could pave the way for the emergence and dominance of financial capital to the detriment of the accumulation process as happened in Chile in the 1970s [*Fortin, 1979, 1984, forthcoming; Griffith-Jones, in this volume*]. This observation is reinforced by consideration of the role of credit market controls.

Much of the neo-classical criticism of the ISI strategy concerns extensive parametric and pervasive state intervention in credit markets, leading to the argument that a less visible hand with minimal parametric intervention would be better equipped to allocate scarce investment funds. There is much force in this argument, since obviously complex and pervasive credit controls and subsidies make it very difficult to unravel exactly what the final effects of credit policy will be. However, the demonstration that one set of credit policies and controls are ineffective or counterproductive does not prove that the parametric intervention and the invisible hand alone will be better. This is so for two reasons. First, because the specific mechanisms for the allocation and control of credit are usually closely connected with reproduction of particular fractions of capital and form an important part of the relationship between capital and the state. In the case of South Korea, the state could, and has, exerted coercion over capital, not just labour. There will be no necessary correlation between reliance on parametric intervention and the invisible hand in credit markets on the one hand, and the use of state power to underwrite more generally favourable Social Conditions of Accumulation on the other, as the disastrous Chilean experience after Allende suggests (see Foxley [*1980*] and O'Brien [*1981*]). In sharp contrast to the dominance of industrial capital in the South Korean and Taiwanese cases, the post-Allende case shows the consequences of the domination of financial capital interests [*Fortin, 1979, 1984, forthcoming*]. Rather than explaining the slow post-Allende recovery through the *ex post facto* revelation of continued price distortion, implying policy error [*Agarwala, 1983: 37*], it would seem that the dominance of financial capital in the 1970s failed to produce an accompanying SSA which was favourable to growth. Thus, the lack of success of the Chilean experiment may be attributed to the consequence of seeing the operation of the price mechanism in abstraction from the SSA. The deviation of Chile from the price distortion–growth relationship shown in Figure 1, taking into account our recalculated distortion index, strikingly illustrates the point.

More generally, any credit money system, either national or international, is ultimately dependent upon state power for the reproduction of the credit system and the enforcement of the function of lender of the last resort. In the international sphere, this problem is most evident in the demise of the gold standard and Bretton Woods exchange system and the removal, first of Britain and then the US as the dominant capitalist states [*Brett, 1982, 1983*]. Current debates over the creation of an international lender of the last resort (see, for example, Lipton and Griffith-Jones [*1983*]) raise these issues even more sharply. Nationally, the character of any credit system and its mechanisms of operation cannot be entirely divorced from the analysis of the state as is often suggested by the neo-classical approach, which is why IMF conditionality is so hotly contested. Indeed in the South Korean case, far from the state retreating from pervasive intervention at the end of the first phase of ISI and concentrating on getting the prices right – a policy which we might assume to involve a significant real rate of interest across the board on capital – precisely the opposite case occurred. Not only did the state continue to direct sectoral investment by instituting different credit regimes, but in many cases the real rates of interest remained highly selective and negative [*Sen, 1981: 298; Hong, 1979: Ch. 6*].

A final area where political economy considerations are of considerable importance is in the characterisation of the role of the MNCs, and processes underlying the choice of techniques and technological transfer. Here, markets are either very imperfect or non-existent leaving a great deal of room for discretionary and interventionist state policies. This much will not be in dispute. What is more contentious is the extent to which state policy should become actively involved in directly setting up the institutional arrangements (state ownership, joint ventures, parastatals and so on) to facilitate the execution of its policies, rather than relying solely on the indirect benefits of market-orientated policies elsewhere in the economy. For example, there is evidence of a more pervasive directive and controlling function of the state in defining and regulating the role of foreign capital in South Korea, particularly in the 1960s and 1970s [*Ensor, 1981; Westphal et al., 1981: 16-22*]. Similarly state institutions were heavily involved in the development of dynamic comparative advantage [*Bienefeld, 1982: 41 and 51*].

To summarise the political economy argument, it would seem to us that the image of state-capitalist economies with EOI and a strong SSA fits the evidence from South Korea and Taiwan rather better than the neo-classical view of a relatively liberal economic order guided by the national policy intervention of a catalytic state and that this has major implications for the generalisation of their experience to other LDCs.

SOME IMPLICATIONS OF THE NIC EXPERIENCE AND ITS POTENTIAL FOR
GENERALISATION

In assessing the NIC experience, neo-classical and World Bank opinion has
been overwhelmingly favourable and has argued strongly for its generalisation. It is argued that difficult and nasty though the process of competition
on the world market might be, especially in the 1980s, the alternatives to a
continued liberal international order are worse. Indeed there are some
strands of the neo-Marxian thought which support such a view, arguing that
the historically progressive role of capitalism is not yet a spent force [War-
ren, 1980; Emmanuel, 1981]. We have raised some doubts with regard to the
generalisability of these policy prescriptions, but rather than trying to reach
a definite conclusion on this complex issue we propose to close the discussion
by considering further the problem of the Social Structure of Accumulation.
The concept of socially necessary exploitation is often used in the Marxian
tradition in order to try and capture the idea that a historical transition from
one exploitative social system to another may bring with it considerable
material and social benefits [Roemer: 1982, Ch. 4]. Thus, in some important
aspects, capitalism is a more progressive social form than feudalism. Socially
necessary exploitation deals with the contradiction between the importance
of struggle against any form of exploitation and the observation that at the
same time the possibility for individual and social development may be
greater under that form of exploitation than an alternative set of social
arrangements. Obviously, such a concept is difficult to apply and especially
open to criticism if applied in an uncritical and linear fashion. Here, we use
the concept in relation to the specification of alternatives to EOI in the state
capitalist NICs. Many forms of exploitation are important under the state
capitalist NICs, both internal (state-capital and labour) and external
(exploitation of nations or Unequal Exchange). What, then, are the forms of
exploitation which are dominant in the NICs, and to what extent can they be
seen as socially necessary?

If comparisons are made with the conditions of labour under developed
capitalism, there is little doubt that the EOI state capitalist NICs are highly
exploitative internally and have been crucially dependent upon direct and
ugly forms of state and military intervention in order to underwrite their
success. Externally, the NIC strategy has recently faced an underlying
increasing Unequal Exchange, witness the unfavourable shift in the terms of
trade between manufactures and imported energy in the 1970s.[15] However,
worsening terms of trade matter little when there is rapid accumulation,
growth and technical change. In relation to alternatives, the relations of
external Unequal Exchange (whether increasing or decreasing) will tend to
continue regardless of the form of social organisation. State-capitalist forms
of continued ISI or Export Promotion have not provided a better basis for
offsetting the effects of unfavourable external conditions, witness the debt
crisis in several Latin American NICs compared with South Korea and
Taiwan. In comparison with other alternatives available, the position is not
clear on at least three counts.

First, the rapid development of the forces of production under EOI in the state capitalist NICs has had substantial material and other benefits to the working population, particularly in the model East Asian cases. On this count, a plus. Second, the many real and potential benefits of the alternative socialist development strategies have had severe costs imposed by super-power rivalries both militarily and in terms of the models of socialist development exported from the existing socialist countries [*Nove, 1983; White et al., 1983*]. In comparison with these alternatives, some aspects of the NIC experience may now be looked upon rather more favourably in the light of the post-war experiences than appeared to be the case in the 1960s. Finally, the difficulties encountered in establishing viable intermediate regimes have been great, leading to disillusionment in experimentation with non-aligned alternatives to EOI in the state capitalist NIC model of development.

If our argument at this stage tends towards an assessment of EOI in the state capitalist NICs as historically progressive, what of the prospects for the 1980s, both for new and existing EOI in state capitalist NICs? Here our position is more equivocal, as is Sutcliffe (in this volume). First, in relation to new state capitalist EOI, given the lack of highly favourable world market conditions which characterised the long post-war boom, the difficulties in generalising the conditions required for successful state capitalist EOI will be greater and the associated degree of exploitation much greater. For the developed capitalist economies more intense competition on the world market in the context of high unemployment potentially threatens the position of labour. In the absence of close and direct participation of working-class organisations in the adjustment process, it is more difficult to see the historically progressive role of capitalism in the same period. Second, the socially necessary forms of exploitation required to allow sustained accumulation at the periphery of the world economy are a direct consequence of specific concrete social processes, each with its own historical momentum. As such, they may not be open to policy choice, hence limiting the generalisability of EOI on the lines of the state capitalist NIC model. Finally, more intense competition on the world market, in the context of high levels of unemployment in the developed economies, directly threatens the position of labour in these economies. This may encourage an increasing trend in technological change which has restored rich-country comparative advantage in some previously labour-intensive commodities which had been successfully exported from the NICs [*Kaplinsky, 1984a; Leontief, 1983*].

NOTES

1. Various elements of this neo-classical story can also be found in Krueger [*1978, 1983*], Bhagwati [*1978*], Balassa [*1980*] and Little [*1981*].
2. The most comprehensive analysis of the neo-classical theory of protection can be found in Corden [*1974*].
3. Most of the natural resources and heavy industry were located in North Korea at the time of partition of the country. The South was left with light industry, agriculture and the bulk of professional groups, many of whom had fled southwards by the end of the Korean War.

4. Neo-classical economics can be '... characterised by *subjective individualism, naturalism* and the primacy it awards to *exchange*' [*Rowthorn, 1974: 64-8*]. One of the consequences of these limited perspectives is a very superficial description of economic phenomenon. In the case of neo-classical [General Equilibrium] Theory, '... the most obvious explanation, why one studies [General Equilibrium] Theory which is known to conflict with the facts, is that one is not engaged in description at all' [*Hahn, 1973: 323*]. The relative lack of interest in descriptive power in neo-classical economics contrasts sharply with its highly developed prescriptive apparatus. Exemplification of this tendency in the analysis of trade policy can be found easily [*Corden, 1974*].

5. One of the most influential developments in the neo-classical analysis of state intervention stems from Krueger [*1974*]. Her analysis of the political economy of the rent-seeking society has behind it an impeccable line of reasoning in economic analysis. Just as Ricardo argued that rent on agricultural land can be an important barrier to accumulation, Krueger argues that the rents created by state control can have similar effects. The new thrust in Krueger's argument is her explicit account of the resource costs in competing for such rents. It is noteworthy that all the state interventions identified by Krueger are at the level of circulation – import quotas, regulation of taxes, minimum wage legislation, interest rate ceilings, and capital gains taxes. The view of a free-trading market economy against which the rent-seeking behaviour is analysed is completely asocial. It ignores the many forms of struggle for control which must develop within any or all of the labour processes which lie behind the free-market outcome. For example, class struggle around the control of the labour process itself has been a very important part of the development of capitalism: historically, the state has been drawn in as a mediator, arbiter and controller of various forms of struggle at the point of production, particularly over the length and conditions of the working day. These remarks are not meant to deny the force of the Krueger argument. Rather, we argue that her use of the standard neo-classical assumptions limits her analysis of the forms of control which may give rise to rent-seeking behaviour and biases her argument against the state as a controller. This bias arises since the free-market economy is posed as a perfectable form of organisation of economic life which functions without any direct forms of control.

6. As Stephen Hymer once remarked it was the invention of the factory system itself which was the key to the changes in the world economy from the eighteenth century onwards, and not the inventions or attraction of markets which were associated with the rise of world trade.

7. For an elaboration of this necessarily brief discussion see Mainwaring [*1979a*], Parrinello [*1979*] and Evans [*1984*]. It is important to bear in mind that in discussing the cost of labour power, the analysis must necessarily also focus on the social relations implicit in the determination of the price of wage goods, such as those embodied in factory production, petty commodity production, household manufacture and so on.

8. If one includes inter-temporal time preference in the determination of savings behaviour and the rate of profit, an explanation of how the preference functions of capitalists or workers are moulded and framed is required. The Cambridge or Kaleckian view has in mind a distinct set of social processes which govern preference formation of capitalists and workers based on both subjective and objective considerations. This does not readily lend itself to portrayal through a generalised preference function which is one of the reasons why this analytical device is often eschewed in favour of a simpler, and potentially less mystifying, determination of the rate of profit outside of the economic model.

9. Empirical support for this proposition is difficult to provide, but the work of Cardoso [*1980: 94-101*] on Brazil, also a state capitalist NIC, strikingly confirms a priori reasoning. See also Taylor [1979: Ch.7].

10. The remarks on the South Korean bureaucracy are based on Michell [*1984, forthcoming*]. See also World Bank [*1983: 68, Box 7.3*].

11. In 1938 Japanese investors owned 90 per cent of the total paid-up capital of all Korean corporations, a figure which fell only marginally to around 85 per cent in 1945 [*Henderson, 1968: 97*].

12. Compare this for example to Zambia which, at independence in 1964 had only 100 university graduates and 1,000 secondary school graduates!

13. For a classic account of this process in the US steel industry, see Stone [*1975*].

14. See, for example, Elson and Pearson [*1981*] and Lipietz [*1982*]. In a slightly different

context, Cowen [*1983*] provides a very useful analysis of the role of capital and the state in the control of household production for primary commodity exports.
15. See World Bank [*1983: 10, 13, Tables 2.3 and 2.4*]. Of course, this does not necessarily translate into adverse terms of trade for any particular NIC, since the composition of trade varies enormously from country to country. For our paradigm NICs, the terms of trade did not decline uniformly throughout the period. In 1981, South Korea's terms of trade stood at 67 (1975 = 100) [*World Bank, 1983: 165, Table 9*].

REFERENCES

Agarwala, R., 1983, 'Price Distortions and Growth in Developing Countries', World Bank Staff Working Papers, No. 575, Washington: International Bank for Reconstruction and Development.

Balassa, B., 1980, 'The Process of Industrial Development and Alternative Development Strategies', World Bank Staff Working Paper No. 438, Washington: International Bank for Reconstruction and Development.

Balassa, B., (ed.), 1982, *Development Strategies in Semi-Industrial Economies*, Baltimore: Johns Hopkins University Press.

Bell, R.M., 1983, 'Technical Change in Infant Industries: A Review of Empirical Evidence'; mimeo, Brighton, Science Policy Research Unit, University of Sussex.

Bhagwati, J.N., 1978, *Foreign Trade Regimes and Economic Development: The Anatomy and Consequences of Exchange Control Regimes*, Cambridge, Mass.: Ballinger.

Bienefeld, M., 1982, 'The International Context' in M. Bienefeld and M. Godfrey (eds.), *The Struggle for Development*, Chichester: Wiley & Sons.

Bowles, S. *et al.*, 1983, 'The Social Structure of Accumulation and Profitability in the Post-War US Economy', Amherst: Department of Economics, University of Massachussetts, Working Paper, January.

Bradby, B., 1983, 'Plan, Market, Money: A Study of Circulation in Peru', unpublished D. Phil. thesis, Brighton: University of Sussex.

Brett, E.A., 1982, *International Money and Capitalist Crises: The Anatomy of Global Disintegration*, London: Heinemann and Boulder: Westview.

Brett, E.A., 1983, 'International Banking and the Crisis: The Problem of Sovereign Debt', mimeo, Brighton: University of Sussex.

Brighton Labour Process Group, 1977, 'The Capitalist Labour Process', *Capital and Class*, No. 1, Spring, pp. 3-26.

Bukharin, N., 1972, *Imperialism and the World Economy*, London: Merlin Press.

Cardoso, E.A., 1980, 'Brazilian Growth and Distribution in the 1960's: An Identity-Based Postmortem', in Taylor *et al.*, [*1980: Ch. 4*].

Caves, R.E. and R.W. Jones, 1981, *World Trade and Payments*, Boston: Little Brown.

Corden, W.M., 1974, *Trade Policy and Economics Welfare*, Oxford: Clarendon Press.

Cowen, M.P., 1983, 'Change in State Power, International Conditions and Peasant Producers: The Case of Kenya', mimeo, London: City of London Polytechnic.

Dhatta-Choudhuri, M.E., 1981, 'Industrialisation and Foreign Trade: The Development Experiences of South Korea and the Philippines in E. Lee (ed.), *Export-Led Industrialisation and Development*, Geneva: International Labour Office.

Elbaum, B., W. Lazanick, F. Wilkinson and J. Zeitlin, 1979, 'The Labour Process, Market Structure and Marxist Theory', *Cambridge Journal of Economics*, Vol. 3, No. 3, pp. 227-30.

Elson, D. and R. Pearson, 1981, 'The Subordination of Women and the Internationalisation of Factory Production' in K. Young *et al.*, *Of Marriage and Market*, London: CSE Books.

Emmanuel, A., 1972, *Unequal Exchange: A Study in the Imperialism of Trade*, London: New Left Books.

Emmanuel, A., 1981, *Appropriate or Underdeveloped Technology*, London: Wiley.

Ensor, P., 1981, 'South Korea's Relationship with Japan in the 1970s. Structural Integration and Dependency in a context of very High Growth and Rapid Adjustment', unpublished M. Phil. thesis, Brighton: Institute of Development Studies, University of Sussex.

Ethier, W., 1979, 'The Theorems of International Trade in Time-phased Economies', *Journal of International Economics*, Vol. 9, No. 2, pp. 225-38.

Evans, H.D., 1984, 'A Critical Assessment of Some Neo-Marxian Trade Theories', *Journal of Development Studies*, Vol. 20, No. 3.

Fei, J.C.H. and G. Ranis, 1964, *Development of a Labour Surplus Economy*, Homewood, IL: Richard O. Irwin.

Fortin, C., 1979, 'The State and Capital Accumulation in Chile in J. Carriere (ed.), *Industrialisation and the State in Latin America*, Amsterdam: Centre for Latin American Research and Documentation.

Fortin, C., 1984, forthcoming, 'Chile: The State and Capital Accumulation' in C. Fortin and C. Arglade (eds.), *The State and Capital Accumulation in Latin America*, London: Macmillan.

Foxley, A., 1980, 'Stabilization Policies and Stagflation: The Cases of Brazil and Chile', *World Development*, Vol. 8, No. 11, pp. 887-912.

Frank, C.R., K.S. Kim and L. Westphal, 1975, *Foreign Trade Regimes and Economic Development*, Cambridge, Mass.: Ballinger.

Galenson, W. (ed.), 1979, *Economic Growth and Structural Change in Taiwan*, Ithaca: Cornell University Press.

Gerschenkron, A., 1966, *Economic Backwardness in Historical Perspective*, Cambridge: Harvard University Press.

Griffith-Jones, S. and E. Rodriguez, 1984, 'Private International Finance and Industrialisation of LDCs', *Journal of Development Studies*, Vol. 21, No. 1.

Hahn, F., 1973, 'The Winter of Our Discontent', *Economica*, Vol. XL, pp. 322-30.

Hamilton, C., 1983, 'Capitalist: Industrialisation in East Asia's "Four Little Tigers"', *Journal of Contemporary Asia*, Vol. 13, No. 1, pp. 35-73.

Henderson, G., 1968, *The Politics of the Vortex*, Cambridge, Mass.: Harvard University Press.

Hong, W., 1979, *Trade Distortions and Employment Growth in Korea*, Seoul: Korean Development Institute.

Jones, L.P. and I.L. Sarkong, 1980, *Government Business and Entrepreneurship in Economic Development: The Korean Case*, Cambridge, Mass.: Harvard University Press.

Jones, R.W., and P.B. Kenan (eds.), 1984, *Handbook of International Economics*, Vol. 1, Amsterdam, North-Holland.

Kalecki, M., 1967, 'Observations on Social and Economic Aspects of "Intermediate Regimes"', *Coexistence*, Vol. 4, No. 1, pp. 1-5, reprinted in M. Kalecki, *Essays in Developing Economics*, Hassocks: Harvester Press.

Kaplinsky, R., 1984a, 'The International Context for Industrialisation in the Coming Decade' in *Journal of Development Studies*, Special Issue on Industrialisation.

Kaplinsky, R., 1984b, forthcoming, 'Indigenous Technical Change: What can we learn from sugar processing', *World Development*.

Kindleberger, C.P., 1962, *Foreign Trade and the National Economy*, New Haven and London: Yale University Press.

Krueger, A.O., 1974, 'The Political Economy of the Rent Seeking Society', *American Economic Review*, Vol. LXIV, June, pp. 291-303.

Krueger, A.O., 1977, 'Growth, Distortions and the Pattern of Trade among Many Countries', Princeton: Princeton Studies in International Finance No. 40.

Krueger, A.O., 1978, *Foreign Trade Regimes and Economic Development: Liberalization Attempts and Consequences*, Cambridge, Mass.: Ballinger.

Krueger, A.O., 1979, *The Development Role of the Foreign Sector and Aid, Studies in the Modernization of the Republic of Korea, 1965–77*, Cambridge, Mass.: Harvard University Press.

Krueger, A.O., 1983, 'Trade Politics in Developing Countries', Seminar Paper No. 249, Institute for International Economic Studies, University of Stockholm, also in Jones and Kenan [*1983*].

Lal, D., 1983, *The Poverty of Development Economics*, Hobart Paperback 16, London: Institute of Economic Affairs.

Lee, T.H. and K. Laing, 1982, 'Taiwan', in Balassa [*1982: Ch. 10, 310-50*].

Leontief, W., 1983, 'Technological Advance, Economic Growth, and the Distribution of Income', *Population and Development Review*, Vol. 9, No. 3.

Lipietz, A., 1982, 'Towards Global Fordism'? *New Left Review*, 132, pp. 33-59.

Lipton, M. and S. Griffith-Jones, 1983, 'International Lenders of Last Resort: Are Changes

Required?', SIFTS/Background Paper, London: Commonwealth Secretariat.

Little, I.M.B., 1981, 'The Experience and Causes of Rapid Labour-Intensive Development in Korea, Taiwan, Hong Kong and Singapore, and the Possibilities of Circulation' in E. Lee (ed.), *Export-Led Industrialisation and Development*, Geneva: International Labour Office.

Luedde-Neurath, R., 1983, 'Import Controls and Export-Oriented Development: A Re-examination of the South Korean Case: 1962–1982', unpublished D. Phil. thesis, Brighton: University of Sussex.

Mainwaring, L., 1979a, 'A Neo-Ricardian Analysis of International Trade' in Steedman [*1979a*].

Mainwaring, L., 1979b, 'On the Transition from Autarky to Trade' in Steedman [*1979a*].

Metcalfe, J.S. and I. Steedman, 1979, 'The Non-Substitution Theorem and International Trade Theory' in Steedman [*1979a*].

Metcalfe, J.S. and I. Steedman, 1981, 'On the Transformation of Theorems', *Journal of International Economics*, Vol. II, No. 2, pp. 267-72.

Michell, T., 1984, forthcoming, 'Administrative Traditions and Economic Decision Making in Korea', *IDS Bulletin*.

Murray, R., 1975, 'The Internationalisation of Capital and the Nation State', in H. Radice (ed.), *International Firms and Modern Imperialism*, Harmondsworth: Penguin.

Nove, A., 1983, *The Economics of Feasible Socialism*, London: Allen & Unwin.

O'Brien, P., 1981, 'The New Leviathan: The Chicago School and the Chilean Regime, 1973–80', *IDS Bulletin*, Vol. 13, No. 1, pp. 38-51.

Ohlin, B., 1932, *Interregional and International Trade*, Cambridge, Mass.: Harvard University Press.

Parrinello, S., 1979, 'Distribution, Growth and International Trade' in Steedman [*1979a*].

Ranis, G., 1981, 'Employment, Income Distribution and Growth in the East Asian Context: A Comparative Analysis', paper presented at Conference on Experiences and Lessons of Small Open Economies, Santiago, Chile, November.

Roemer, J.E., 1982, *A General Theory of Exploitation and Class*, Cambridge, Harvard University Press.

Rowthorn, R., 1974, 'Neo-classicism, Neo-Ricardianism and Marxism', *New Left Review*, July-August.

Samuelson, P.A., 1975, 'Trade Pattern Reversals in Time-Phased Systems and Inter-temporal efficiency', *Journal of International Economics*, Vol. 5, No. 4.

Schmitz, H., 1983, 'Technology and Employment Practices: Industrial Labour Processes in Developing Countries', Brighton: Institute of Development Studies, University of Sussex.

Sen, A.K., 1981, 'Public Action and the Quality of Life in Developing Countries', *Oxford Bulletin of Economics and Statistics*, Vol. 93, No. 4.

Smith, M.A.M., 1984, 'Capital Theory and Trade Theory', in Jones and Kenan [*1984*].

Steedman, I. (ed.), 1979a, *Fundamental Issues in Trade Theory*, London: Macmillan.

Steedman, I., 1979b, *Trade Amongst Growing Economies*, Cambridge: Cambridge University Press.

Stone, K., 1975, 'The Origins of Job Structures in the US Steel Industry', in R.C. Edwards, M. Reich and D. Gordon (eds.), *Labour Market Segmentation*, Lexington: D.C. Heath.

Sutcliffe, B., 1984, 'Industry and Underdevelopment Re-examined', *The Journal of Development Studies*, Special Issue on Industrialisation.

Taiwan Statistical Data Book, 1982.

Taylor, L., 1979, *Macro Models for Developing Economies*, New York: MacGraw-Hill.

Taylor, L., *et al.*, 1980, *Models of Growth and Distribution for Brazil*, Oxford: Oxford University Press.

Wade, R., 1983a, 'South Korea's Agricultural Development: The Myth of the Passive State', *Pacific Viewpoint*, Vol. 24, No. 1, pp. 11-20.

Wade, R., 1983b, 'Agriculture and the Developmental State in Taiwan', research report delivered to IDS Seminar Series on Politics, States and Markets, Autumn term, Brighton: University of Sussex.

Walsh, V.C., and H. Gram, 1980, *Classical and Neo-Classical Theories of General Equilibrium*, Oxford: Oxford University Press.

Warren, B., 1980, *Imperialism: The Pioneer of Capitalism* (ed.), J. Sender, London: Verso.

Westphal, L., *et al.*, 1981, 'Korean Industrial Competence: Where it Came From', World Bank Staff Paper No. 469, Washington: International Bank for Reconstruction and Development.

White, D.G., *et al.*, 1983, *Revolutionary Socialist Development in the Third World*, Brighton: Wheatsheaf.

White, D.G., 1984, 'Developmental States and Socialist Industrialisation in the Third World', *Journal of Development Studies*, Special Issue on Industrialisation.

Williams, J.H., 1929, 'The Theory of International Trade Re-Considered', *Economic Journal*, reprinted in H.S. Ellis and L.A. Metzler, *Readings in the Theory of International Trade*, Illinois: Irwin.

World Bank, 1983, *World Development Report*.

APPENDIX

Price Distortions and Growth

Consider briefly the discussion of the relationship between price distortions in general and economic growth in the 1983 World Development Report [*World Bank, 1983: Ch. 6*] and in the key background paper [*Agarwala, 1983*]. It is concluded that one-third of the variation in growth performance of 31 developing countries (only some of which would be classified as NICs) can be explained by a composite index of price distortion. The main results of this study are reproduced in Figure 1.

The general argument behind Figure 1 is simply that, *ceteris paribus,* price distortions hinder growth through a wide variety of mechanisms. The cross-section results obtained are robust in the sense that alternative methods of aggregating the individual indexes yield broadly the same result. Thus, whilst the average growth of GDP for the 1970s for the countries shown was about five per cent, low price distortion could yield about two per cent p.a. growth extra and high price distortion two per cent p.a. less. In reaching this conclusion, some care is taken, particularly in Agarwala [*1983: 37 and 46*] in separating the argument for the removal of price distortion from an argument for *laissez-faire*.

There are a series of methodological issues which arise when attempting such exercises, acknowledged to some extent by the authors themselves. It will be apparent from the discussion in the text that the theoretical definition of undistorted prices for capital and labour will be contentious, though in the case of trade distortions there is likely to be a wide measure of agreement. As noted by Agarwala [*1983: 34*], there is a major conceptual problem in assessing the relative importance of different types of distortion and relating these to effects on growth. Here, perhaps the most that can be usefully said is that, in general, the neo-classical perspective is likely to exaggerate the negative consequences of price distortions (however measured theoretically) because so many of the social and political factors which, as we shall see, are used to explain the deviations around the regression, are *ab initio* abstracted from the very construction of the theory of price. Putting aside

FIGURE 1

PRICE DISTORTIONS AND GROWTH IN THE 1970s

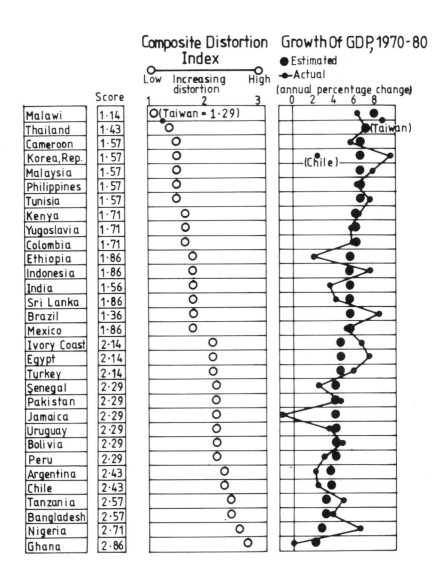

Source

[*World Bank, 1983: 62, Figure 6.1*] and [*Agarwala, 1983: 36, Figure 1*]. In this figure countries are listed in order of increasing degree of distortion of prices. In the first section, the score on a composite index of distortion covering seven components – foreign exchange rate, protection of manufacturing, protection or taxation of agriculture, the pricing of capital and labour, power these theoretical issues, what of the empirical estimates of the price distortions themselves?

The most striking quality of the Agarwala estimate of price distortion is the degree of subjectivity of some key parts of the exercise. We will take three examples. First, consider the index of foreign exchange distortion, which Agarwala [1983: 19] argues has a stronger association with growth than any of the other price distortions considered. Yet the empirical criterion relates to a separation of countries according to the degree of appreciation in the relative exchange rates during the 1970s. Presumably this is done on the grounds that distortion induced through government intervention is likely to overvalue the exchange rate. However, it would seem absurd to automatically classify an exchange rate appreciation induced by the oil boom (for example, in Nigeria and Indonesia) as price distortion in any meaningful sense. Second, again on foreign exchange rate distortions, it would appear to be quite inconsistent to argue that Chile experienced a high degree of distortion on the grounds that there was a high distortion at the beginning of the 1970s and high fluctuations after an initial adjustment. The fact that there was a radical change from high protection and therefore high distortion of manufactures prices to low protection in 1974 did not prevent a classification of low protection for the whole period, and there appears no good reason not to use the same judgement for the foreign exchange market. The conclusion is reinforced by the observation that for the latter part of the decade the fluctuation in the average real exchange rate was only about six per cent, which is not very high when compared, for example, to Bangladesh during the same years which is given a low foreign exchange distortion index. Third, looking at the distortion index for Chile in the labour and capital markets, it would seem contentious to define these as having high distortion. Fortin [1984, forthcoming: Tables 4.9, 4.15 and 4.A3] suggests that real wages did not recover to 1970 levels during the whole decade, that there are serious discrepancies between official and independent estimates of the decline in returns to labour, and that alternative estimates of the real rate of interest show very high real rates of interest. In Figure 1, we have recalculated the composite distortion index assuming low price distortion for the foreign exchange, capital and labour markets in order to highlight the consequences of a radically different interpretation of post-Allende Chile.

---

tariffs and inflation. The middle section graphs the composite index of price distortion. The small circles in the right-hand section show the actual annual rate of growth of GDP. The large circles are estimates of GDP growth obtained by a regression relating to the distortion index. The alternative estimates of the value of the distortion index for Chile and the additional estimates for Taiwan were calculated by the authors. For Chile the modified index assumed a low distortion for the foreign exchange rate, the pricing of labour and the pricing of capital. The reasoning behind these alternative classifications is given in the text. For Taiwan, the composite index was constructed as far as possible using the same criterion as adopted by Agarwala using various sources, including Galenson [1979], Lee and Laing [1982] and the Taiwan Statistical Data Book 1982, together with the assistance of Robert Wade. The individual scores were: foreign exchange, low; manufacturing protection, low; protection/taxation of agriculture, medium; price of capital, medium; price of labour, low; power tariffs, low; inflation, low. Assigning low = 1, medium = 2, high = 3, the composite index is 1.29.

Whilst we have questioned individual estimates for some of the price distortions indexes used in Figure 1, we do not dispute the overall conclusion that price distortions do matter. Of greater interest for our purposes is the explanation of the major deviations from Figure 1. In Table 1 we have listed those countries noted to have large deviations from the explained variance in Figure 1 noted by Agarwala [1983: 43].

TABLE 1

NON-PRICE EXPLANATIONS OF GROWTH

Large positive deviation		Large negative deviation	
Country	Explanation	Country	Explanation
South Korea	institutional/ political	Ethiopia	political
Brazil	institutional	Jamaica	political
Ivory Coast	technical and financial assistance	Ghana	political
Indonesia	oil	India	institutional
Egypt	oil	Chile*	institutional
Nigeria	oil		

Source: Agarwala [1983: pp. 43, 44]

*Author's estimates and judgement.

What is striking about Table 1 is the extent to which vaguely defined institutional and/or political factors are introduced to explain the major unexplained deviations from predicted growth performance taking into account price distortions. In terms of the categories used in this paper, it is the SSA which needs to be examined more carefully. Yet it would be a mistake to argue that it is only necessary to introduce the SSA to explain the deviant cases. For example, it would be highly misleading to argue that institutional and political factors were not extremely important in the case of Taiwan, which is not a deviant case in terms of the price distortion–growth relationship in Figure 1. Just as Bradby [1983] notes in relation to the Spanish Conquest of Peru, where the Inca's highly planned and centrally co-ordinated social system was mistaken for a market economy, so it is with much of the neo-classical literature that treats the market as a social force independent of the SSA.

Private International Finance and Industrialisation of LDCs

by Stephany Griffith-Jones and Ennio Rodriguez *

The relationship between external finance and industrial growth in Less Developed Countries (LDCs) is complex. Nevertheless on the basis of the experience of many LDCs over the 1970s it would appear that, together with an interventionist state, external financial flows have been instrumental in rapid industrialisation. During this period substantial net financial resources were made available to LDCs by the private banking system. Although these loans carried high interest rates they were associated with low conditionality. However in the current period the debt problems of the Third World have made the banking system reluctant to provide additional resources, giving a pronounced role to the IMF and the World Bank in shaping the terms on which (reduced) financial resources are provided. These new loans are associated with high levels of conditionality which, inter alia, may have a negative impact on industrial growth. The argument is sustained in this paper through an analysis of changing aggregate financial flows, and short case studies on Chile and Brazil.

I: INTRODUCTION

Developing countries are prone to facing foreign exchange constraints in their development processes. International financial inflows can thus finance expenditure beyond domestic resources. If this capital is used for developmental processes gross fixed capital formation can be accelerated, and this can be particularly important in increasing the pace of industrialisation. Although most economic theorists and development practitioners accept that external capital is necessary for accelerating growth and industrialisation, it must be recognised that there is little consensus about their exact inter-relationship.[1]

In Latin America there has been a wide spectrum of views on this subject. Amongst those most critical of the role of external capital because of its potential negative effects on national autonomy have been analysts linked to the 'dependencia' school. For example, Sunkel [1969] wrote: 'It is in this aspect ... the overbearing and inevitable necessity to obtain external financing ... which finally sums up the situation of dependency; this is the crucial mechanism of dependency'. It is noteworthy that Sunkel – in common with other, though not all radical thinkers – reluctantly recognised the need for

* The authors are respectively at the Institute of Development Studies at the University of Sussex, and the School of Economics, University of Costa Rica. They would like to thank Raphie Kaplinsky and Hubert Schmitz for their valuable comments on an earlier draft.

external capital for industrialisation and development, despite being critical of its effects. On the other side of the spectrum, other theorists have not only asserted categorically the need for external capital in development, but have tried also to quantify through a relatively simple mathematical model the optimal flows of external capital to a developing country; an early influential study along these lines was that of Chenery and Strout [*1966*], which was based on a 'two gap' (that is, foreign and domestic saving) model. Although this approach helped to highlight the role of external capital in development, it was criticised for its excessive and almost mechanical emphasis on foreign exchange as the sole constraint on development, and its concentration on the aggregate level – with its corresponding neglect of sectoral considerations. An intermediate position on the relationship between external capital and development can be found in the writings of Raul Prebisch [*1964, 1979*]. Prebisch argued that acceleration of the rate of growth of developing countries implies more than a proportionate increase in the demand for imports, as a tendency to external disequilibrium is inherent in the process of development, particularly in the context of industrialisation. This process accelerates the demand for imports of manufactured and other goods, creating a serious bottleneck that, if not overcome, may inhibit development. Prebisch attributes a useful role to a transfer of foreign financial resources *provided* they are taken in conjunction with other measures (both at a national and international level); that the volume and conditions of such flows are appropriate to the countries' development needs; that such flows are sustained during long periods; and that they are used for investments which will contribute to an increase in exports and/or the substitution of imports.

However, it is important to recognise that the nature of the link between external capital and development cannot be discussed in merely abstract terms, since it is linked to the precise form in which foreign financial flows are transferred. This reflects both the nature of the agents who generate these flows, and the financial and other terms on which such flows take place. In each of the decades after World War II a new actor arose, whose financial flows to developing countries played a major or dominant role in providing international finance. In the 1950s it was the foreign investors pursuing greater profits which provided the main source of finance. During the 1960s official aid agencies played the most dynamic role as, in this decade, aid was perceived to be in the interests of industrial countries, particularly the US. During the 1970s, the most dynamic actors were the multinational banks which rapidly expanded their lending to several developing countries in search of greater profits. Even though partly responding to the needs and pressures from developing countries, the main motive for these flows was naturally that they were perceived as serving the best interests of the agents carrying them out.

One of the most problematic aspects in the world economy of the 1980s seems to be the lack of a new actor willing and able to play a dynamic role in the financing of the Third World. At the same time the institutions which did play a dynamic role in former decades (namely, official aid agencies, TNCs, and multinational banks) seem unwilling to continue to do so to the same extent as in the past. The only institution which has in the early 1980s substantially increased both its lending as well as its ability to encourage other agents to increase their flows, is the International Monetary Fund (IMF). There are, however, two major problems with this trend. First, the contribution of IMF net lending is still relatively small compared with the size of LDCs' current account deficits, and it is not clear to what extent this level can be sustained in the near future given constraints on the funds available to the IMF. Second, and perhaps more important, IMF lending in the upper credit tranches is associated with a type of conditionality which can not only be considered undesirable from a particular country's point of view, but which more broadly seems to introduce an important deflationary bias in the world economy[2] and arguably inhibits long-run industrial strategies (see Kaplinsky in this volume).

The aim of this article is twofold, first, to raise the issues involved in an evaluation of the impact of the development of private international lending to LDCs on their industrialisation and, secondly, to look at their prospects in the 1980s in the context of an absence of a new actor willing and able to provide adequate finance to LDCs. In pursuing this discussion we do not necessarily give primacy to the link between external finance and industrialisation. Other facts (such as market access, explored in other chapters of this volume) may be of equal or even greater importance. Moreover, the relationship will clearly vary between countries and over time. Yet the issue remains a crucial – and underexplored – one, and it is for this reason that we proceed with what must inevitably be an initial and tentative analysis.

II: THE 1970s AND PRIVATE INTERNATIONAL BANKS

Major Features of International Financial Flows

There are six major features of the flow of international finance over the 1970s, a period of sustained export-led industrialisation in the Third World:

(a) The 1970s have witnessed a sharp deterioration of most oil importing developing countries' terms of trade and at the same time a rapid build-up of gross domestic capital formation which outstripped the increase in gross domestic savings (see, for example, UNIDO [*1980*]. Consequently, the current account deficit of all oil-importing developing countries is estimated to have increased more than threefold in real terms during the period 1970–80. In order to sustain such a high deficit, total external flows to deficit developing countries increased dramatically, at an estimated growth of 9.0 per cent per annum in real terms during 1970–80 (see Table 1).

(b) A second important trend which emerged very clearly during the 1970s was that credit flows to deficit developing countries became increasingly 'privatised'. Private medium- and long-term credits which represented only 37 per cent of total net capital flows to the Third World in 1970

TABLE 1

OIL IMPORTING DEVELOPING COUNTRIES:
FINANCING CURRENT DEFICITS, 1970–80 (BILLIONS US$)

	Level	(Current Prices)	Annual Percentage Growth (Constant Prices)
	1970	1980	1970–80
Current account balance	-8.6	-69.6	(12.1)
Financed by:			
1. Net capital flows	9.1	55.3	9.0
a) Total aid (grants and concessional loans)	3.1	16.3	7.5
b) Medium and long-term borrowing	4.3	33.4	16.6
Official export credits	0.5	2.6	7.2
Multilateral	0.5	3.2	9.4
Private	3.4	27.5	19.7
c) Private direct investment	1.7	5.6	2.7
2. Change in reserves and short-term borrowing	0.5	14.3	

Source:World Bank, *World Development Report 1981*, Table 5.3.

had grown to 50 per cent of those flows by 1980, as they increased at an estimated average annual rate of about 20 per cent (see Table 1).

(c) It is interesting to note that foreign direct investment – which until the early 1970s had been the main source of private financial flows to the Third World – grew slower than other forms of external capital during the 1970s, and therefore declined rapidly in importance; as a source of financing current account deficits of oil importing LDCs, direct investment declined from about 20 per cent in 1970 to 10 per cent in 1980. With the expansion of commercial bank lending, the financing of foreign direct investment in developing countries itself changed, as the financing needs of transnational companies were covered increasingly from sources other than equity from

TABLE 2
THE PATTERN OF GLOBAL CAPITAL FLOWS (a)
(IN BILLIONS OF DOLLARS)

	1967–73(b)	1974–77(b)	1978	1979	1980
Group of ten countries and Switzerland	–8.25	–0.75	–19.25	23.25	51.50
Smaller developed countries	1.50	17.75	10.50	12.00	22.00
Non-oil developing countries	6.00	21.00	22.50	36.00	51.00
Oil export- ing countries	–1.25	–38.00	–4.50	–68.00	–116.00

Notes: (a) Minus signs indicate capital export.
      (b) Annual averages.

Source: A. Lamfalussy. 'Changing attitudes towards capital movements'. BIS, 1981, based on OECD and IMF data.

parent companies, relying increasingly on financing from local banks or the Euro-currency market.

(d) Most of the growth of private bank lending to the Third World occurred through the so-called Euro-currency market, and took the form of syndicated loans with floating interest rates.

(e) Another important feature of international financial flows during the 1970s was that there was a tendency for OPEC countries to replace the industrial countries as the main net suppliers to the rest of the world (and therefore to the developing countries). This trend, shown in Table 2, is an important departure not only from the 1950s and 1960s, but also from earlier periods, when the industrial countries were the main net suppliers of financial flows to the rest of the world. This trend was obviously reflected in the net flows of Western private international banks, which played an important role in the recycling from surplus to deficit countries during the 1970s.

(f) A noteworthy feature in the 1970s was the relatively small quantitative role played by the International Monetary Fund in the financing of oil-importing countries' current account deficits; in fact, during several years in the late 1970s the Fund's net financial flows to developing countries were negative, as repayments exceeded gross loans. This is widely recognised to have been caused by two factors. First, IMF quotas as a percentage of non-oil developing countries' trade declined sharply after the late 1960s, and the ratio of Fund quotas to those countries' current account deficits declined even faster. As a result, the Fund's capacity to provide balance of payments assistance, particularly unconditionally, or with low conditionality, declined substantially. Second, developing countries' willingness to borrow from the

IMF, particularly under its high conditionality programmes, declined significantly during the 1970s, as countries increasingly resisted the conditions on their economic policy attached to such loans; moreover, at this time they had ready access to unconditional private bank loans.

The Significance of Euro-Market Lending to Developing Countries

International banking and lending have grown rapidly since the early 1960s. The Euro-markets are the international capital markets specialising in borrowing and lending currencies outside the country of issue. These have grown at a steady and spectacular rate since the mid-1960s. The net size of the narrowly defined Euro-currency market which was less than US$100 billion in 1972, reached almost US$600 billion by 1980. However, if the *gross* claims in the broadly defined Euro-currency market are considered, then the total exceeded US$1,000 billion by 1980 [*Bank for International Settlements, 1981*]. At the same time as the Euro-currency market expanded at a very rapid pace, the proportion of its loans going to developing countries grew very substantially, and by mid-1982, about a third of external bank assets were estimated to be directed towards them [*Johnson, 1982*].[3]

The factors which led to such a high proportion of international lending being orientated towards developing countries during the 1970s have been discussed in detail elsewhere (see *Griffith-Jones, 1980*). Of particular relevance here is the fact that international banks were keen to lend to developing countries as the credit demand from their traditional clients in the industrial countries slowed because of the recession. At the same time deposits from oil exporters and other sources were growing very fast and this prompted the banks to lend to borrowers previously considered as marginal. Besides the need to finance rapidly growing current account deficits, at a time when net aid flows grew very slowly, many Third World governments seemed to prefer foreign private loans both to official credits and to direct investment, partly because the former were perceived as generating a lesser degree of dependence, thus allowing greater autonomy for the national government.

The development of new operational techniques in the Euro-currency market, particularly during the early 1970s, allowed a reduction in risk for the individual Euro-banks making these loans to developing countries, particularly those with the long maturities preferred by developing countries. First, the 'roll-over credit' was created, based on a floating interest rate that varied (approximately) with the lenders' cost of money obtained on the essentially short-term inter-bank market. The base rate for these loans to the developing countries was often LIBOR (London Inter-Bank Office Rate), or the US prime rate, which are measures of the cost of funds to the banks. Thus, although loans to the developing country may have had a long maturity (e.g., ten years), the interest rate changed every time the credit was rolled-over (usually every three or six months). This floating interest rate, as it is called, is crucial because it passes on to the borrower one of the most important risks of the market and it is the borrower who is exposed to both cyclical and long-term changes in interest rates. Second, a very large part of the transactions of the Euro-currency markets by developing countries have been through syndicated loans. These loans, which originated in the late 1960s, are credits shared by a large number of Euro-banks. This mechanism has allowed the default risks of large loans to be spread over a great number of banks; at the same time it also allowed smaller banks to participate in the Euro-currency markets.

Without a doubt, the large volumes of private lending to developing countries played an important role during the 1970s. However, private bank lending as a major source of finance to LDCs posed serious problems, both for the developing countries and the banks themselves. These problems, although already noted by some observers in the late 1970s, have become much more acute and widely recognised recently (see Section III below). Here we will point out two important aspects: (a) the concentration of bank lending, and (b) its high and variable cost.

A major limitation of commercial bank lending during the 1970s lay in its distribution. Private banks clearly preferred lending to developing countries with relatively high per capita income, as well as to those whose recent growth record was more impressive. Poor countries (both in income levels and/or natural resources) were not considered to be sufficiently 'credit-worthy' to attract significant flows. As a result, private bank lending was heavily concentrated among the upper- and middle-income developing countries. As a result, the four largest borrowers (Mexico, Brazil, South Korea and the Philippines) accounted for well over 60 per cent of total accumulated debt of non-OPEC, non-OECD developing countries to inter-national banks in December 1982 (based on data in BIS [*1983*]). Low-income countries are estimated to have obtained only 2.6 per cent of total net lending to oil-importing developing countries in the period 1972–80.[4] In fact, low-income LDCs actually can be said to be net lenders to the private international banks, as their reserves deposited with those banks exceed the loans received [*Killick, 1980*]. Lending was also very highly concentrated geographically, as an extremely high proportion of lending to LDCs went to Latin America and particularly to Brazil, Mexico, Venezuela and Argentina.

A second problem of commercial lending to developing countries was that the terms of the loans were less favourable than those of other sources of finance, and less appropriate for the financing of countries' development. On average, maturities for private loans are significantly shorter than those for official loans. This implies that they are much less appropriate for financing projects (such as some industrial ones) where the gestation or 'infant' period tends to be very long. Furthermore, the cost of borrowing privately (particularly through the syndicated roll-over loans, which have characterised Euro-market lending to developing countries), has been on average higher than the official flows; even more problematic is the variability (and hence lack of predictability) of the interest rate paid on contracted loans. This variability adds an important element of uncertainty in developing countries' attempts to predict and plan their future balance of payments flows. Moreover, as a result of rapid increases in the rates of interest in industrial countries since 1979, the gap between interest paid on commercial loans with floating interest and that paid on fixed interest had increased substantially.

As can be seen in Table 3, the floating interest costs of developing countries more than doubled from *8.2 per cent* of their outstanding debt in 1971–73 to an estimated *18.0 per cent* in 1981. As an effect of rising interest rates and of the increasing 'privatisation' of financial flows (with a higher proportion of floating rate debts), the cost of servicing interest as a proportion of total exports of goods and services rose rapidly for LDCs (see Table 4). The low-income countries were much less seriously affected than the others, as they borrow so little on the private markets. The most seriously affected by these trends were Brazil and Mexico, whose gross and, particularly net borrowing, in variable interest loans has been so steep that the net transfer of resources to developing countries (which is the proportion of borrowed funds available for buying imports and increasing reserves, after amortisation and interest payments) declined sharply as a proportion of gross borrowing, from 50 per cent in 1975–76 to 22 per cent in 1980.

TABLE 3

INTEREST COST OF OIL IMPORTING DEVELOPING
COUNTRIES' OUTSTANDING DEBTS (AVERAGE PERCENTAGE RATE)

	1971–73	1974–78	1979	1981
Fixed interest (a)	4.0	4.4	4.9	5.2
Floating interest (b)	8.2	9.3	12.3	18.0
Total	4.8	5.9	7.2	9.5

Notes: (a) Interest payments during the year as percentage of total outstanding debt, all
expressed in US$.
(b) Estimated total cost, including spreads and fees.

Source: *OECD Development Assistance Review. 1981.*

TABLE 4

INTEREST PAYMENTS AS PERCENTAGE OF
EXPORTS OF GOODS AND SERVICES

Interest Payment Ratio	1973	1975	1977	1979	1981
All non-oil LDCs	4.4	4.8	4.6	6.5	7.2
Low-income LDCs	3.1	2.8	2.7	3.0	3.4

Source: IMF. *World Economic Outlook. 1981.* Table 30.

III: FINANCIAL FLOWS AND INDUSTRIALISATION STRATEGIES IN THE 1970s

The changing patterns of external financial flows coupled with increases in volume during the 1970s posed important questions. To what extend did larger financial flows and their growing 'privatisation' augment the options open to *some* developing countries, and to what extent did they place new constraints on policy-making and on the nature of industrial development? Did the changing nature of these financial flows affect the autonomy of the state in Third World countries and hence influence their participation in the industrial sector?

Relatively little analysis has been done on the impact of rapidly changing financial flows on industrialisation. We shall attempt here some preliminary comments on this subject, considering, *inter alia*, the type of conditionality attached to different types of financial flows and the impact of external finance on the industrialisation strategies pursued during the 1970s. We believe that these points are best illustrated by reference to the experience of individual countries, and we thus consider briefly the cases of Brazil and Chile. Both had abundant access to private finance during this period, but pursued significantly different industrial strategies with contrasting success. Whilst each of these countries had differing industrial capabilities and backgrounds, with varying natural endowments and size we believe that it is nevertheless possible to draw from their experience some conclusions with respect to the historic relationship between industrialisation and external finance. Their experience is also of some relevance to the industrialisation of developing countries over the coming decade.

Financial Flows and Conditionality

Historically, official loans and aid were granted mostly for specific projects particularly in the case of multilateral agencies such as the World Bank and the Interamerican Development Bank. Their evaluation and surveillance were mainly undertaken in technical terms and the use of funds was also closely monitored. Resources were allocated following sectoral priorities. Increasingly, however, official flows have also established programme loans for general balance of payments purposes. The criteria are either similar, or linked to IMF criteria (for example, the World Bank Structural Adjustment Loans). In both this project and programme lending, the criteria for lending were predominantly influenced by the donor governments and not only reflect prevalent trends in development thinking in the lending agencies, but also the socio-political models advocated by the donor countries. Thus, during the late 1960s and 1970s, stress was placed on financial criteria. During the 1970s, greater emphasis was placed on export promotion as the main engine for growth and development.

The dominant type of financial flows in the 1970s (private credits from multinational banks) had a rather different content. In practice these funds were seldom tied to specific projects, and in those cases where they were, banks neither monitored actual expenditure nor carried out technical evaluation of the projects. Furthermore, there was no theorisation on development or growth behind the lending policies of private banks, who seemed to be less overtly political in their criteria than official institutions. This was because they did not serve so closely the political interests of their 'home' country or countries, nor were they influenced by their legislatures; they confined themselves to the pursuit of 'profitable business'. Their main criteria for lending decisions was the profitability and security of their loans; they preferred to lend to countries from whom they could obtain higher margins and/or to those which they perceived as being more clearly committed to debt repayment and more able to do so. As a result their emphasis tended to lie on short-term indicators. Great stress was placed on the balance of payments and variables such as the rate of inflation, the level of foreign exchange reserves and trade balances. It is noteworthy that the rate of investment to GDP (arguably a rough indicator of medium-term economic prospects) was barely considered of importance to determine 'creditworthiness'. In critical situations the banks demanded, as a precondition for granting further loans or restructuring existing ones, that the country sign a standby agreement with the IMF, as has been seen with a score of countries in the most recent (1982–83) period.

Industrialisation and Private Financial Flows

The evidence in Table 5 suggests that changes in the growth of import capacity were positively associated with overall economic performance and growth of manufacturing production in developing countries during the mid-1970s. Those countries that had lower import capacity during 1973–76 when compared with the period 1965–73 also experienced a decline in average rates of growth of GDP, total domestic investment and manufacturing

TABLE 5

IMPORT CAPACITY AND ECONOMIC PERFORMANCE OF NON-OIL DEVELOPING COUNTRIES (UNWEIGHTED AVERAGES OF AVERAGE ANNUAL PERCENTAGE GROWTH RATES)

	30 Countries With Sustained Or Improved Growth of Import Capacity (a)	40 Countries With Diminished Growth Of Import Capacity (b)
Gross Domestic Product		
1965–73	4.3	4.9
1973–76	5.3	2.9
Domestic Investment		
1965–73	6.1	5.3
1973–76	15.3	4.3
Manufacturing Output		
1965–73	6.8	7.2
1973–76	5.7	3.3

Notes: (a) Countries having an annual rate of growth of import volume in 1973–76 equal to or greater than that experienced during 1965–73.
(b) Countries having an average annual rate of growth of import volume in 1973–76 below that experienced during 1965–73.

Source: Dell, S., and Lawrence, R., 1980.

output, while countries where the growth rates of imports during 1973–76 equalled or were higher than those of 1965–73, recorded average rates of growth of GDP and investment well above the earlier period. Manufacturing output grew in the latter group at a slightly lower pace than in the previous period; nevertheless, the slowdown is less than in the case of the countries with diminished import capacity and the rate of growth is higher as well.

The association between import capacity, industrial growth and export performance is a complex one for which there are a number of (not necessarily exclusive) explanations. To a certain extent a relatively rapid increase in sustained industrial growth was also positively associated with a growth in export earnings. It is possible therefore that the imports required for industrial growth were provided by exports. However, the enhanced import capacity also reflected the significant inflow of external financial resources described in Section II; and because of these large financial inflows, some developing countries (particularly those whose exports had been, and were growing rapidly), were able to sustain both net investment in the industrial sector and the import of the intermediate inputs required to sustain or expand industrial output.

On balance it seems that for a number of countries the latter link had greater importance, implying that at least to some extent, the industrial growth of many developing countries in the 1970s was facilitated by the availability of large sums of international finance. In drawing this conclusion we do not (for the moment) offer a view with respect to the durability of this growth (in industrial and other sectors), that is, whether it enabled developing countries merely to put off the structural adjustment necessitated by changes in the terms of trade and world recession (a view increasingly influential since the late 1970s in certain orthodox circles), or whether it was an important stage in long-term growth and industrialisation in the Third World. However, what is significant, as we shall argue below, is that the absence of a major lender of international finance in the coming decade, makes the maintenance of such foreign finance-associated industrial strategies problematic.

In order to substantiate these points, we turn briefly to our analysis of the contrasting industrial experiences of two Latin American countries, Brazil and Chile.[5] Both had abundant access to private finance during this period, but pursued *significantly* different industrialisation (and indeed broader development) strategies, with contrasting success. Whilst each of these countries had differing industrial capabilities and backgrounds, very different natural endowments and, in particular, different-sized internal markets, we believe it is nevertheless possible to draw from their experience some conclusions with respect to the relationship between industrialisation and external finance. These conclusions are likely to be particularly relevant for middle-income developing countries.

Inevitably, given the complexity of the subject, the following comments can no more than raise some of the issues involved in such an evaluation. The discussion is organised around three sets of issues: first, balance of payments and 'creditworthiness'; second, financial intermediation and, third, industrialisation and finance. Finally, some tentative conclusions are drawn on the nature of the relationship between the development of private international finance and industrialisation as they emerge from the two case studies.

Chile

Since 1973 the Chilean military Government has attached top priority to adjusting the economy as rapidly as possible to internal and financial 'disequilibria'. The priority was such that this was often achieved at the cost of growth and development. Furthermore, the short-term policy measures used by the Chilean military Government to achieve this short-term adjustment have always been extremely 'orthodox'.[6] These short-term changes were linked to fundamental restructuring of the Chilean economy, geared towards facing it as much as possible to 'the magic of the market', both nationally and internationally. In the area of foreign trade, the 'model' was geared towards 'opening up' the economy to international competition; for this purpose, tariffs were significantly reduced from a relatively high 94 per cent average in 1973 to a level of 10 per cent in 1979, amongst the lowest in the Third World. A similar 'opening up' occurred in the area of international finance. At the same time, the role of the state in the economy was sharply decreased from its formerly high level; as a result, the share of public investment in total gross domestic investment consistently declined from 75 per cent in 1970 to 30 per cent in 1981 [*Fortin, forthcoming*] (based on official Chilean Government sources). As the role of the state diminished and as policy was dominated by short-term macro-economic considerations, there was no clear vision of a development or industrialisation strategy for the Chilean economy, except in that it should rely as much as possible on 'market forces'.

(a) Balance of payments and general economic evolution: The decade after the military coup saw three distinct periods in relation to the balance of payments. In the first period of 'shock treatment' to restore financial equilibrium (which began in 1974 and accelerated in early 1975) there was a collapse of industrial and total production and a relatively low net inflow of medium- and short-term private capital. The economy only started to recover after 1977 (the second phase) coinciding with an increase in the net inflow of private credits. However, these credits were used mainly to finance additional imports, rather than in increasing reserves; this not only led to problems in the balance of trade but to competition with existing industries, many of which went bankrupt as a result of this competition. Exports increased, but particularly since the late 1970s, did so at a lower rate than imports, hence leading to an increasing trade balance deficit. Finally, in the late 1970s net capital inflows (particularly from private banks) increased and some of this was used to build up foreign exchange reserves.

Borrowing in the Euro-currency markets in the Chilean case was thus clearly associated with an expansion of imports since 1977 and particularly after 1979. Moreover, consumer goods which in 1974 accounted for 28 per cent of total imports, had risen to 38 per cent by 1981 [*Banco Central, 1983*].

Many of these imported consumer goods were luxury goods, whose import had been previously prohibited. Furthermore, the rapidly mounting deficit in the services of the current account was a reflection of the increasing interest that had to be paid to service the rapidly growing foreign debt at high interest rates. By 1981, the deficit on the services account almost reached the size of the trade deficit (see Table 6).

TABLE 6

CHILE: BALANCE OF PAYMENTS, 1974–1981 (MILLIONS OF CURRENT US DOLLARS)

	1974	1975	1976	1977	1978	1979	1980	1981
Current account	−211	−491	148	−551	−1189	−1189	−1971	−4814
Balance of trade	357	70	643	34	−355	−355	−764	−2598
exports	(2151)	(1590)	(2116)	(2185)	(3835)	(3835)	(4705)	(3960)
imports	(−1794)	(−1590)	(−1473)	(−2151)	(−4190)	(−4190)	(−5409)	(−6558)
Services	−579	−571	−523	−660	−914	−914	−1320	−2316
Capital account	218	240	199	572	2247	2247	3165	4769
Direct foreign investment	−17	−4	−1	16	233	233	170	376
Autonomous capital	235	244	200	556	2014	2014	2995	4393
Balance of payments	−55	−344	414	113	1047	1047	1244	70

Source: Banco Central de Chile. *Boletin Mensual*. July 1983.

(b) Financial intermediation: Of almost all developing (and developed) economies in the 1970s, the Chilean financial system probably underwent the most profound transformation during the 1970s [*Schneider, 1980*]. Not only were the external sources of finance 'privatised', but so were their internal counterparts. In 1974 the Chilean private sector accounted for 11 per cent of total medium- and long-term debt; by 1981 its participation had risen to 65 per cent [*Goni, 1983*].

This increasing importance of the private sector in the financial system is a crucial element in the change of the development strategy after the *coup d'etat*. It required a series of legal reforms which enabled Chile to have by 1978 the most liberalised financial system in Latin America [*Schneider, 1980*]; interest rates were 'freed' which led to real interest rates equivalent to a significantly higher level than the return on productive activities. This had far-reaching implications. The State was undermined as the major allocator of resources, and by 1978 the private *financial* sector had become increasingly concentrated and expanded its activities to most spheres of the economy. The priorities in the allocation of funds came thus to be determined to a very large extent by a small group of private interests, dominated by financial speculators for whom the acquisition of productive enterprises was only a temporary way to maximise return on their liquid funds. The logic of economic decisions was thus stood on its head; financial resources were no longer an input into production; on the contrary productive investment became an instrument to generate short-term liquidity, which could generate far higher profit by their subsequent deposit in the financial system or through the purchase of new enterprises. The predominance of 'speculative' investment over productive investment was reflected in a rapid decline in the rate of investment, as a percentage of GDP. At the same time, the Chilean state not only lost its leading role as 'investor', but as planner and designer of the development and industrialisation strategy. The market (and particularly the 'financial market') determined the allocation of short- and long-term resources, and therefore the adjustment and development strategies.

(c) Industrialisation and finance: Chilean industrial production is estimated by different sources to have declined at an annual rate of between −0.5 per cent and of −3.1 per cent during 1972–82 [*Foxley, 1983*]. Consequently the share of the industrial sector in total production declined from 25.5 per cent in 1974 to 18.9 per cent in 1982 [*Foxley, 1983*], (based on official sources). These figures give support to the statement that in reality the strategy has turned out to be one of de-industrialisation. This seems more clear when comparing the Chilean decline of industrial production during the 1974–82 period with an average growth of industrial output for Latin American countries of 3.8 per cent, and 4.6 per cent for all developing countries during that same period. Furthermore, in the same period industrial employment *declined* in Chile at an average annual rate of −5.9 per cent, while in Latin America as a whole it expanded at an annual rate of three per cent. It has been estimated that between 1974 and 1982, 200,000 jobs were 'destroyed' in the industrial sector; this estimate is based on a comparison between observed levels of employment and levels of employment that would have existed, had historical trends been sustained [*Foxley, 1983*].

The Chilean 'model' was particularly *vulnerable* to fluctuations in the world economy, given that it had opened itself so rapidly and so completely both to foreign trade and to foreign financial flows. A combination of factors hit the Chilean economy badly, namely, the decline in world trade growth since 1979, the significant deterioration of the terms of trade which practically all oil-importing developing countries suffered since 1979, and the sharp reduction in net private capital inflows to Chile (as to most Latin American countries) particularly since 1982, accompanied by high international interest rates. Even more than in the mid-1970s, the Chilean Government's response in the early 1980s was based on 'automatic adjustment', which basically implied very restrictive macro-economic policies leading to a dramatic recession, which according to Chilean official sources is reported to have experienced a decline of 15.5 per cent in GDP during 1982 [*Banco Central, 1983*].

As discussed above, the expansion of the financial system was very large; the share of GDP generated in banking is estimated to have almost tripled, from 4.3 per cent in 1973 to 11.0 per cent in 1982! [See *Fortin, Table 4, A.2*]. In the early post-*coup* period (1973–76), interest rates were freed for non-banking financial institutions which underwent a rapid process of growth and centralisation. Later, as interest rates for the whole financial system were freed, the financial groups previously strengthened gained control over the banking system and very extensively over the dynamic sectors of the economy. Net investment (as proportion of GDP) was particularly low in the

1975–79 period, recovering slightly afterwards but still remaining at very low levels, both in comparison with previous Chilean levels and with the Latin American average.

Transformation of property structures and reorientation of industry to the export market implied other important changes. Interests associated with the import-substituting industrial structure (both capital and labour) were virtually destroyed and, hence, these largely ceased to play a role in the determination of economic policies. The interests linked to foreign trade and particularly to financial capital tended to predominate and benefited from their expansion into the dynamic sectors of the economy [for a detailed discussion, see *Fortin, forthcoming*].

Brazil

The Brazilian 'model' of growth and industrialisation differs in important aspects from the Chilean one. In the first place, during the 1970s the Brazilian Government placed far higher priority on sustaining growth and industrialisation than the Chilean one, even in the face of severe internal and external financial disequilibria; the priority given to financial equilibria was clearly quite low during the 1970s. Furthermore, both in short-term management and in long-term growth and industrialisation strategies, the Brazilian Government was much more pragmatic than the Chilean one, relying far less dogmatically on market forces (e.g. by sustaining or even increasing during certain periods the level of public investment, and by the use of tariff barriers and other forms of control over trade).

(a) Balance of payments and general economic evolution: The evolution of Brazil's balance of payments differs significantly from that of Chile. A major increase in foreign borrowing took place during the 1974–75 oil shock so as to avoid recession and both long-term and short-term borrowing increased. (Net capital transfers in the capital account in 1974 were nearly double the 1973 figures.) Although the steady growth of exports and the improvement in the terms of trade turned the trade balance into surplus in the following years, the invisible trade deficit rose continuously after 1974; so, too, did Brazil's foreign indebtedness.

The second rise in the price of oil rekindled a trade balance deficit which was once again met with increased indebtedness, so that import capacity was not affected and high growth rates were initially maintained, especially in the industrial sector. But unlike the earlier period, world recession and declining terms of trade hit the value of Brazilian exports after 1981. The high level of debt as well as high international interest rates also hit Brazil's service account very badly. Consequently after 1982 external finance ceased to be available to mop up the ever-increasing current account deficit.

(b) Financial intermediation: In contrast to Chile, the weight of the Brazilian private sector in the total foreign debt had not exceeded one-third [*Lessa, 1980*]. This figure correlates with the importance of the state and state enterprises in the development strategy [*Lessa, 1980*]. Access to the

Euro-currency markets by the public sector and the use made of these funds largely responded to explicit development goals. Although the private financial sector grew, it did not acquire a dominant role as in Chile, due to its more gradual liberalisation and due to the increased importance of state investment.

(c) Industrialisation and finance: The overall expansion of Brazilian output was very impressive throughout the 1970s (see Table 7), such that the growth of GDP was well above that of most developing countries and well above that of the industrial countries. This was equally true for the industrial sector, reflected in its annual growth rates (see Table 7) and in the very rapid expansion of the share of manufactures in total exports, from 21 per cent in 1971 to 42 per cent in 1980 (see Table 8). Even in years when private investment declined, total investment did not due to the increase in state investment; the latter's share in total fixed investment is estimated to have grown from 38 per cent in 1970 to 43 per cent in 1978 [*Castro-Andrade, 1982*]. Of particular importance since the mid-1970s has been the expansion of public enterprises into heavy industries. The expansion into new productive sectors by the state has been helped by the large flows of private credits which the Brazilian Government and state enterprises were able to obtain on the Euro-markets, and also by the rather unique participation of the Brazilian state in the national financial and monetary systems. Besides the

TABLE 7

BRAZIL: AVERAGE ANNUAL GROWTH RATES OF GDP (1971–1981)

	GDP	Agriculture	Industry
1970–73	11	5	13
1974–78	7	5	8
1979–80	7	6	7
1981	–4	7	–8

Source: Bekerman, M., forthcoming. Based on Fundacao Gertulio Vargas. *Conjunctura Economica*. December 1981.

TABLE 8

BRAZIL: VALUE OF EXPORTS

MAIN GROUPS, 1971 AND 1980 (PERCENTAGES)

	1971	1980
Coffee	29	14
Other primary products	42	34
Semi-manufactures	8	10
Manufactures	21	42
TOTAL	100	100

Source: Banco Central do Brasil. *Boletin Mensual*.

budgetary resources, the activities of the state in the open market have provided a large source of funds [see *Castro Andrade, 1982*].

Furthermore, the Brazilian response to the deterioration in the international environment and the subsequent deterioration in the trade balance which occurred since 1974 was radically different to that of the Chilean Government. Instead of basically relying on deflation to control the level of imports, an alternative which the Brazilian government explicitly rejected [see, for example, *Bekerman, forthcoming*], it preferred to control imports. A variety of mechanisms were used including the prohibition of imports of 'superfluous' items, increases in tariffs, high deposits on many imports, and additional incentives towards import substitution. It is noteworthy that this increase in protection coincided with (and did not seem to be in contradiction to, as would be argued in orthodox circles) an expansion of exports, which included an increase in the share of industrial exports. In Brazil, the use of policies, which subsidised certain types of exports as well as more general tax rebates on goods exported, helped compensate the negative effects which increased protection on imports had on export competitiveness.

Although Brazil was very successful during the 1970s in maintaining high levels of growth, its record is much less impressive in terms of the broader aspects of development. In particular, a relatively small proportion of its expanding resources was devoted to the provision of social services [*World Bank, 1979*]. This was particularly serious given that Brazil is one of the countries with the most inequitable income distributions in the world [*World Bank, 1981*].

When after 1979 Brazil, like other oil-importing LDCs, was affected by deterioration in the international environment, a decision was made to try to avoid the recessionary alternative at all costs, which meant resort to increased external indebtedness. Emphasis was placed on short-term policies, with sophisticated manipulation of the financial system used to avoid pursuing the recessionary option. However, particularly after the 1982 debt crisis, Brazil was forced to negotiate an agreement with the IMF, which led to increased emphasis on economic policies that were of a severely deflationary nature (even though still significantly less so than the Chilean one for the same year). In the short term this recession naturally affected the industrial sector, as well as potentially endangering future industrial growth due to a decline in industrial investment.

Some Comments on Industrialisation Strategies and their Linkage to International Finance

The availability of external finance to some LDCs opened for them new possibilities as well as potential pitfalls, the outcome of which depended upon the development strategies pursued by these countries. Thus, the impact of the availability of foreign finance on these strategies cannot be divorced from the evaluation of the strategies themselves.

Considerable differences in the strategies of development and in the use made of external finance can be observed between Brazil and Chile. In the latter, increased foreign borrowing coincided with a decline in the rate of investment as a proportion of GDP, and with a very poor performance in the 1974–82 period. External finance was largely spent on consumption of imported goods, many of them of a 'superfluous' nature. In contrast Brazil used private external funds in an attempt to sustain or even increase its level of investment, and was able to maintain almost as high rates of growth after 1973 as it had in the 1967–73 period.

Thus, in the Chilean experience, the overall economic policies and strategy adopted meant that private foreign credits on the whole contributed both to (a) de-industrialisation by financing imports which competed with national production, particularly in the industrial sector and by helping sustain an overvalued exchange rate during several years in spite of growing trade deficits, and (b) to accelerate the trend towards a more unequal pattern of income and consumption. The latter consequence arose because of two factors. The first one was the high proportion of cheap luxury imports. The second was because of the development of a two-tier capital market. Here the external private capital market, mainly used by large enterprises, operated at international interest rates while the internal capital market, with prohibitively high interest rates, had to be used by small and medium industrial entrepreneurs who had no access to international credit and whose profits were eroded by the prohibitive interest rates charged by the Chilean financial institutions [see *Herrera, 1979*].

This does not constitute a critique of the impact of private financial flows on developing countries in general, but rather a comment on their impact in the context of the type of model pursued by the Chilean Government, which implied 'freeing' market forces in international trade and finance as well as in internal capital markets, and reducing the role which the state traditionally had in the Chilean economy. Chilean Government officials in the late 1970s often argued that it was this 'free-market' model which made the country attractive to foreign bankers. Yet, as we have shown elsewhere [*Griffith-Jones, 1981*], this belief – which in fact helped increase internal support in Chile for the more orthodox positions – was already inconsistent with facts. During the 1970s private bankers – although possibly having some preference for free-market governments – lent large sums to well-established socialist countries as well as to capitalist countries which pursued far less orthodox policies than did Chile (as, for example, was the case of Brazil).

Given the results of the Chilean transition to 'pure capitalism', the important question arises as to whether if other countries were to follow a similar route, similarly negative consequences could be expected. The question is particularly relevant because orthodox defenders of the free market, including influential representatives of official international financial institutions (whose influence is increasing) consistently advocate a similar path for different types of developing countries, including low-income ones, with very frail industrial sectors.

Although mechanical comparisons are always difficult, it would seem likely that similar problems would arise in other countries as have occurred in Chile as a consequence of a drastic and rapid freeing of 'the magic of the free market'. These effects would probably be more clearly negative in countries where, as in Chile, the state had previously played an important role in development and where the economy had grown with relatively high levels of protection; it is to be feared that they would also probably be even more negative in poorer countries, whose incipient industrial sectors could be more vulnerable to sudden and total exposure to market forces. These statements are of necessity tentative, and by no means imply a rejection of the crucial role which we believe market forces must play in development. It is rather that an analysis of the Chilean experience seems to confirm what Van Arkadie [1983] concluded in another context that 'for the policy maker, the market is a useful servant but a poor master'. The Chilean experience, as well as similar ones during the 1970s in other countries of the Southern Cone of Latin America, would also seem to reinforce rather strongly the need for greater humility by international financial institutions in their recommendations, particularly in their advocacy of the 'free market' as an optimum tool for adjustment and growth in developing countries.

The Brazilian experience during the 1970s (as well as that of other middle-income developing countries such as South Korea, and of industrial countries such as Japan), seems to show that the contribution of foreign capital inflows is more positive for overall growth and industrialisation if: (a) it is regulated; (b) it occurs in an economy where the state has a clear 'vision' of a development strategy, and in which the state sector plays an important role in investment (both directly through state enterprises and indirectly through incentives to the private sector to invest productively); and (c) where deliberate policies are pursued by the state to orientate market forces (for example, in international trade and finance, as well as in internal capital markets) towards sustained growth in specific productive sectors (selective protectionism being an important instrument in this sense).

On industrialisation issues, the experience of the 1970s would suggest that pragmatism in policy-making seems more fruitful than orthodoxy of any kind. For example, even though it may be desirable to reduce excessive levels of protection in particular developing countries, it is counter-productive for growth for this to be done abruptly and at a time of severe balance of payments crisis, as was done by the Chilean authorities in the mid-1970s. A more gradual redirection of protection, which can be temporarily reversed in case of a severe foreign exchange crisis – as has been done in Brazil and South Korea – seems much more beneficial for sustaining growth, particularly in the industrial sector.

The Brazilian experience in the 1970s also shows that some middle-income countries could achieve important successes in the field of export growth and diversification (particularly towards industrial exports). Even though this required a battery of policies geared towards export promotion, it did not seem to require – as orthodox analysts would claim – substantial liberalisation of imports.

These tentative conclusions should not however be extrapolated mechanically to other periods (e.g. the 1980s) in which the conditions of the international economic environment – and in particular the growth of world trade and of net financial flows to LDCs – seem to be far less favourable for export-led and debt-sustained 'models' of industrialisation and development than was the case in the 1970s.

Vulnerability of growth – particularly in the industrial sector – to fluctuations in international trends is therefore not only a feature of 'models' like the Chilean one, even though such pure 'models' are far more vulnerable to such fluctuations, as the dramatic decline in Chilean output since 1981 has shown. It also applies – though to a lesser degree – to countries such as Brazil, which have attempted a more pragmatic and gradual 'opening up' of their economies to trade: given a more significant role for the state sector; and which have relied heavily on substantial net foreign finance and expanding foreign markets to sustain such growth. Within the international environment of the early 1980s, it unfortunately seems difficult to force the continued success of these strategies of industrialisation (as well as of alternative ones) partly due to the reduction in foreign finance available to developing countries. It is to this likely future financial scenario that we will turn our attention to in the next section.

The difficult conditions in the international environment of the 1980s would also seem to reinforce the need for prudence in national financial management, so as to avoid excessive imbalances in the state budget and excessive monetary expansion, which may lead to high levels of inflation and/or problems in the Balance of Payments. Even though 'obsessions' with financial equilibrium lead to very negative effects on the real economy (as is illustrated by the Chilean experience under Pinochet), the opposite attitude of attempting to ignore financial constraints (as to some extent occurred in Brazil, particularly in the late 1970s, and – in a different context – occurred in Chile during the Allende Government) may provoke crisis with very undesirable economic and political effects. In this respect, it may be that the Asian experiences of industrialisation (for example, in South Korea or India) may perhaps provide useful 'lessons' for Latin American countries on how to combine unorthodox industrialisation and development strategies, with prudent financial management.

IV: THE EARLY 1980s AND OUTLOOK: RESCHEDULING, OFFICIAL LENDING
    AND INDUSTRIALISATION

In the early 1980s, new trends emerged in the external financing of developing countries, largely resulting from the vast amount of debt already accumulated by them and from the prolonged recession in the industrial countries. These new trends became much clearer after late 1982; if a precise moment in time were to be identified, it would be the August 1982 Mexican external financial crisis. Much of the lending which has occurred since the turn of the decade (and particularly that by the private international banks) has been reluctant and defensive; as the main February 1983 *Euromoney* article, 'Syndicated lending out for the count', points out clearly, 'Most of the loans [in 1983] will be business the banks don't want to do.'

The Unwilling Lenders: the Private Banks

In fact, since 1979 the growth of private bank lending to non-oil developing countries had been slowing down; as a result the share of net private long-term capital flows in the financing of these countries' current account deficits declined significantly, from its peak of 38.2 per cent in 1978 to 31.6 per cent in 1979 and to 27.5 per cent in 1980 [*IMF, 1982*]. Although the evolution of international liquidity may have played an important role in this slower growth, the main factor has been the perception by the private multinational banks of increased risk in their loans to developing countries.

It is interesting that there were important regional differences in these flows. The gross bank lending which went to Latin American countries after the second half of 1982 was mainly involuntary, and associated with the rescheduling 'package deals'. This was in sharp contrast with loans to Asian developing countries, to which private banks still seemed very keen to provide funds. We may as a result be seeing not just a decline or slower growth in private lending to LDCs, but also a relative shift in geographical distribution amongst them, from Latin American countries to other areas, and in particular to Asian countries. (It is as yet difficult to ascertain how large and how permanent such a shift may be.)

The main reason for this change in attitude of the bankers towards regional distribution is that the size of the external debt of Latin American oil-importing countries – although not high in relation to the level of their total economic activity – is exceedingly high when compared with their export earnings. Furthermore, a far higher proportion of the external debt in Latin America was at variable interest rates (which as we have seen tends to be more costly) than in other LDCs. As a consequence of these trends, according to World Bank figures (which exclude amortisation of short-term debt), by 1982 Latin American oil importers' debt service burden had risen to 53 per cent of exports compared with 8.6 per cent for the South-east Asian oil importers. These higher debt-service payments, added to the increased reluctance of private bankers to continue providing funds, have forced Latin American governments to adopt recessionary policies, so as to cut imports rapidly. In contrast growth in the South-east Asian middle-income countries has held up relatively better. Debt-sustained industrialisation in the South-east Asian middle-income countries may thus offer better prospects, particularly in the short term but perhaps also within a longer-time horizon than in Latin America.

Nevertheless, despite the reluctance of these private banks, several of the large rescheduling packages recently assembled (particularly those of Mexico, Brazil and Argentina) have involved quite significant increases in their lending to those countries; private banks were asked by the IMF to raise their exposure to Mexico during 1983 by eight per cent and to Brazil by approximately 12.5 per cent. In fact, these levels of new lending by the private banks are not being determined by their own autonomous decisions. The new approach to rescheduling involves an unprecedented degree of interaction and collaboration between private banks, the IMF, the Bank for

International Settlements and the governments of industrialised countries. In particular, the IMF and the industrial countries' central banks have in several cases told the private banks by exactly what percentage they must increase their exposure to particular countries. This degree of pressure by international official institutions has no precedent. It has been reinforced by the fact that the IMF has itself refused to agree to lend to a particular country until the private banks have committed themselves to make new loans of a certain size. Many bankers have welcomed the IMF's moves to influence rescheduling of direct commercial credit, and to organise such 'package deals', as they perceive that this diminished the risk of open default by particular countries. Other banks are very critical of this new role which the IMF has assumed. For example, Mr S.M. Yassukovich, managing director of a small but prestigious Euro-market bank, stated that:

> For the first time in our history as independent bankers we have been robbed of our freedom of action in taking a decision on whether to make a loan or not. We have been told that if we don't make a loan, our standing in the market could be prejudiced. It seems to be a fundamental interference with the independence of bankers. If people think through the implications of that they will be horrified. *It is going to accelerate the process of people dropping out of the market* (Financial Times, 15 December 1982) (emphasis added).

The last point seems very crucial. It has, for example, been reported that as a result of IMF pressure on private banks in the Mexican 'package deal', some smaller banks rapidly reduced their inter-bank credit lines to Brazil in anticipation of similar IMF policies. This contributed to the serious financial problems of that country to which we referred above.

A final characteristic of recent lending and rescheduling is the difficulty and complexity of these operations. Not only do official institutions (such as the IMF, BIS and the different central bankers of industrial countries) have to co-ordinate amongst themselves and negotiate with the government of the debtor country, but they also have to reach agreement with a vast number of commercial banks. The complexity of the task also implies that agreement is often delayed beyond the targeted time; the situation is further complicated by the need for new bridging loans. This implies a particularly high level of uncertainty, which makes the design of both long- and short-term economic management more difficult for developing countries' policy-makers.

The Increased Role of the IMF in Lending to Developing Countries

As discussed above, the IMF has since late 1982 played a key role in the process of organising, lending and rescheduling 'package deals' for developing countries. This new role has been accompanied (as well as strengthened) by the increased lending which the Fund itself has been making to developing countries since the beginning of this decade. This contrasts with its very small contribution during the last decade. In 1978, net use of Fund resources by non-oil developing countries had in fact been negative; in 1979 it had increased very marginally; however, in the early 1980s net use of Fund resources by developing countries increased significantly.

One of the main factors which explained the IMF's increased lending in the early 1980s was its relatively greater availability of financial resources. The seventh review of Fund quotas became effective in December 1980, leading to an increase of total Fund quotas from about SDR 40 billion to SDR 60 billion.[7] Furthermore, the IMF borrowed significant sums in the early 1980s: in particular, it entered into a medium-term loan agreement with the Saudi Arabian Monetary Agency for up to SDR eight billion, and a far smaller short-term loan agreement with the central banks and official agencies of certain industrial countries. The Fund's future ability to lend will be further enhanced once the recent agreement (in principle) to increase Fund quotas by 47.5 per cent, is ratified by national governments, particularly by the US.

Demand for IMF credit has been growing, as the possibility of obtaining private credits without the Fund's 'seal of approval' has become much more limited and as the sums available for borrowing from the IMF have become larger. Under the policy of enlarged access, approved early in 1981 and operational till late 1983, countries could borrow up to 450 per cent of their quotas from the Fund to support high conditionality programmes. This was an important increase relative to the situation during most of the 1970s, when a country could usually borrow up to 165 per cent under an extended arrangement, or up to 100 per cent under a standby. However, it should be emphasised that this enlarged access is linked to upper credit tranche, high conditionality programmes (which is in contrast with the mid- and late 1970s when most developing country borrowing from the Fund was through low conditionality programmes). As a result of recent trends in private bank and IMF lending, the issue of appropriate Fund conditionality (and the potential negative impact of current Fund conditionality) on developing countries' growth and industrialisation has become much more crucial. The option of avoiding Fund conditionality by borrowing only from the private capital markets is no longer open even to those countries which were able to follow it in the 1970s (such as Brazil).

Official Flows

The increase in IMF lending to LDCs is in sharp contrast to the evolution of ODA, which in 1981 fell even in nominal terms. With regard to multilateral official flows, however, new measures have been implemented, particularly by the World Bank, which may have some impact on sustaining private capital flows to developing countries at a time when commercial lenders have become very cautious.[8]

Although clearly positive in themselves, such measures may strengthen the leverage which multilateral financial institutions (in this case, the World Bank) exercise over countries' economic policies. This will remain a particular source of concern while there are doubts about whether the policies that these institutions recommend to developing countries are in fact most appropriate to encourage those countries' industrialisation and growth.

Prospects

At the time of writing it seems particularly difficult to make forecasts about future developments in international finance, especially as regards private bank lending to developing countries. One possibility is that dramatic recent changes – both in the private capital markets and in the world economy – will imply a significant reduction in the long-run rate of their growth (possibly transformed into decline) and in the structure of private lending to developing countries, and its distribution among countries. Another possible change involves the mechanisms which will be used for such lending. A third question relates to the link between private banks' lending and the role played by official institutions, in aspects as different as their 'seal of approval', the guarantees they will grant, their co-financing activities and as lenders of last resort facilities.

As mentioned above, one view still stressed by many – though a decreasing number – of bankers, as well as some of the most dogmatic defenders of the 'free market', is that once the recession is over private bank lending to developing countries will continue to operate basically in the same way as it did in the 1970s, albeit at a slower pace. This is reflected in the 'business as usual' attitude still rather influential in banking circles, and the models still used to project private bank lending to LDCs for the 1980s, which use practically the same assumptions as those applied in the past.

Another view, which seems far more realistic, is that structural changes have and are occurring in the international private capital markets. As a consequence, a moderate world recovery will not be sufficient to restore growth in private financial flows to developing countries. This perception is often accompanied by proposals to: (a) reduce and/or redistribute the timing of the amortisation of the LDCs 'debt overhang'; (b) take measures to ensure that future private flows to LDCs can be sustained and are carried out through mechanisms more appropriate to developing countries' and international banks' needs; and (c) create new mechanisms. Currently, a variety of proposals on these aspects are circulating in banking, academic and journalistic circles. Some of these proposals are related to the 'rediscounting' of part of the developing countries' private bank debt.[9]

Such proposals – which would imply some losses for the private banks – would enable the 'rediscounting agency' to stretch out maturities and reduce interest rates for developing countries' debts, without budgetary cost to industrial countries; these proposals are often accompanied by suggestions that future private lending to LDCs should move away from medium-term loans with floating rates to longer-term fixed interest bonds. This latter suggestion (which would be particularly desirable for the financing of mining and industrial projects, with long gestation periods) seems unfortunately unrealistic at a time when short-term lending to LDCs has been proportionately increasing and bond financing to LDCs has been clearly declining. Proposals for 'debt rediscounting' and future more appropriate lending mechanisms to LDCs have been linked to the possible creation of an explicit international lender of last resort facility, which would support banks in case of major developing countries' defaults or other difficulties. This is mainly so as to help sustain banks' lending capacity, thus avoiding the risk of serious deflation which the reduction of lending can have not only on LDCs but on the whole of the world economy [*Lipton and Griffith-Jones, 1983*].

These types of proposals are largely linked to the fear that if measures are not taken to reduce the debt burden of developing countries and to ensure continued appropriate lending to them, developing countries will either be forced to continue to deflate their economies excessively so as to be able to service their debts, or may react to their extremely difficult balance of payments situation, and to socially and politically unacceptable consequences of deflation, by declaring explicit default. The latter option is increasingly becoming part of the political debate in Latin America, even though not explicitly supported by the current governments of the major LDCs debtors. Its attraction may be increased if net transfers of capital continue to be negative for Latin America as they clearly were in 1982, and if such negative transfers imply the need for drastic recession in the national economies.

The fear of default and of its impact on industrial countries' economies may however force new or existing agents to increase net positive financial transfers to developing countries. Industrial countries' private bankers may provide developing countries with unusual support, to the extent that their interests and those of developing countries coincide. As a result, the new dynamic actors in the finance of developing countries may be pushed on the stage, rather than jump on it with enthusiasm, as occurred in previous decades.

As we saw above, easy availability of international financial flows for some middle-income developing countries during the 1970s opened for them both new possibilities as well as potential pitfalls; the effect of this availability of external finance clearly depended on the development strategy pursued by different countries. In Brazil's case, the relatively pragmatic policies pursued by the Government in its industrialisation strategy, in particular in 'orienting' market forces towards growth in specific sectors as well as allowing the state to play an important direct role in investment, implied that the contribution of capital inflows in the 1970s was positive both for growth and industrialisation. In the Chilean experience, the rapid adoption of ultra-orthodox free-market policies by the Government seem to have implied that net foreign lending in fact contributed both to de-industrialisation and to a more unequal pattern of income and consumption. Thus whereas in the Brazilian case foreign finance contributed in the 1970s to sustain industrialisation, in Chile during the post-1973 period foreign finance sustained (or made easier) a strategy which led *de facto* to de-industrialisation – for example, by financing imports of industrial consumption goods, which competed with, and in many cases destroyed, national industry.

In the 1980s, it is likely that *net* foreign financial transfers, even to middle-income countries, will be significantly smaller than they were in the previous decade and that they will be more closely linked to tighter 'conditionality' on the economic policies of developing countries than they were in the 1970s (as agreements with the IMF and/or the World Bank increasingly become a precondition for other types of foreign financial flows). On the basis of the experience of Brazil and Chile during the 1970s, this likely financing scenario gives cause for some concern, particularly with respect to industrial policies and income distribution. For even though the policy advice granted by these two multilateral institutions is not as dogmatically committed to 'ultra-orthodoxy' as was Chilean policy over the 1970s, it would appear that industrial strategies which undermine the role of the state make deindustrialisation more likely. At the same time the likely reduction in foreign finance would suggest, on the basis of recent Brazilian experience, that even with an interventionist state, the maintenance of historic industrial growth rates will be problematic.

Recent instability and unreliability of net financial flows, the conditionality attached to an increasing proportion of these flows, as well as the stagnation of world trade in the early 1980s would seem to recommend that large developing countries' governments rely in the future relatively less in their industrialisation and development strategies on export-led and debt-sustained growth than they did in the 1970s, and emphasise relatively more, to the extent that it is feasible, production for the internal market and reliance on national savings. Such strategies would *de facto* require an important role for the national state to complement and guide the private sector. Smaller developing countries are, however, more limited in the extent to which they can rely on their own internal market.[10] Such countries may have to rely relatively more on export promotion than larger ones; but as we have argued, this does not necessarily imply resort to an 'orthodox' strategy of industrialisation.

NOTES

1. For an early clear review of different positions on this subject see K. Griffin 'The Role of Foreign Capital' and relevant section of Select Bibliography in Griffin (ed.), [1971]; for a more recent review, from a different perspective, see Seiber [1982].
2. For a good critique of IMF conditionality, see Dell [1981].
3. These estimates are based on BIS figures which tend to underestimate lending to developing countries since they do not reflect the lending passing through offshore countries.
4. Estimate based on data in OECD [1981, Table V-6].
5. For an interesting comparison of the Brazilian experience in the 1960s and Chilean experience in the 1970s, which focuses mainly (but not exclusively) on stabilisation policies, see Foxley [1980].
6. On some occasions during the mid-1970s the Chilean Government has even adopted more orthodox measures than those suggested to it at the time by the IMF or the World Bank [see *Griffith-Jones, 1981*]. There are probably very few Third World governments which can 'boast' of such orthodoxy.
7. This increase is substantially less than the increase of 100 per cent suggested by developing countries and the IMF staff itself, but higher than the initial US proposal.
8. In January 1983, the World Bank introduced on an experimental basis, new co-financing techniques which are meant to offer greater security to commercial lenders as well as improving the terms of commercial lending for developing countries, for example, by a lengthening of their maturities, as the World Bank will cover the part of the loan that has the longer maturity.

9. See, for example, ICIDI [*1983, especially pp. 92-5*]; Rohatyn [*1983*], and Mackworth-Young [*1983*].
10. For a more detailed discussion, see Rodriguez [*1983*].

REFERENCES

Banco Central, 1983, several issues *Boletin Mensual*, Chile.
Banco Central do Brasil, 1983, several issues *Boletin Mensual*, Brazil.
Bank for International Settlements, 1983, 'The Maturity Distribution of International Bank Lending', July.
Bank for International Settlements, 1981, *Annual Report*, Basle.
Bekerman, M., forthcoming, in Griffith-Jones, S., and C. Harvey, (eds.), *World Prices and Development*, London: Heinemann.
Castro-Andrade, R., 1982, 'Brazil: The Economics of Savage Capitalism' in Bienefeld, M., and M. Godfrey, *The Struggle for Development: National Strategies in an International Context*, London: Wiley.
Chenery, H., and A. Strout, 1966, 'Foreign Assistance and Economic Development' *American Economic Review*, No. 56, September.
Dell, S., 1981, 'On Being Grandmotherly: The Evolution of IMF Conditionality', *Princeton Essays in International Finance.*
Dell, S., and R. Lawrence, 1980. *The Balance of Payments Adjustment Process in Developing Countries*. United Nations, New York: Pergamon.
Fortin, C., forthcoming, 'The State and Capital Accumulation in Chile', in Anglade C. and C. Fortin, (eds.), *The State and Capital Accumulation in Latin America*, London: Macmillan.
Foxley, A., 1980, 'Stabilisation policies and stagflation: The cases of Brazil and Chile', *World Development*, Vol. 8.
Foxley, A., 1983, 'Un Nuevo Camino Economico', *Hoy*, November, Santiago.
Goni, J., 1983, 'La via chilena al endeudamiento externo', *Research Paper Series*, No. 37, Institute of Latin American Studies, Stockholm.
Griffin, K., (ed.), 1971, *Financing Development in Latin America*, London: Macmillan.
Griffith-Jones, S., 1980, 'The Growth of Multinational Banking, the Euro-currency Market and their Effects on Developing Countries', *Journal of Development Studies*, Vol. 16, No. 2.
Griffith-Jones, S., 1981, 'The Evolution of External Finance, Economic Policy and Development in Chile, 1973–78', *IDS Discussion Paper 160.*
Griffith-Jones, S., 1981, *The Role of Finance in the Transition to Socialism*, London: Frances Pinter.
Herrera, J.E., 1979, 'La inversion financiera externa en los modelos de desarrollo hacia afuera: el caso de Chile, 1974–78', *Cuadernos* CIEPLAN, No. 1, Santiago, Chile.
ICIDI, 1983, *Common Crisis*, The Brandt Commission, 1983, London: Pan Books.
IMF, 1981, *World Economic Outlook, 1981.*
IMF, 1982, *World Economic Outlook, 1982.*
Johnson, C., 1982, 'The International Credit Market', paper presented to the Financial Times/World Banking Conference, 9 December.
Killick, T., 1980, 'Only Select Borrowers Benefit'. *Financial Times*, 7 November.
Lamfalussy, A., 1981, 'Changing attitudes towards capital movements', BIS.
Lessa, C., 1980, 'La administracion de la crisis actual', *Economia de America Latina*, No. 4, March.
Lipton, M., and S. Griffith-Jones, 1983, 'International Lender of Last Resort: Are changes required?' SIFTS/Background Paper, *Commonwealth Secretariat.*
Mackworth-Young, B., 1983, 'Role for International Bond Markets' in 'World Banking', *Financial Times*, 9 May 1983.
OECD, 1981, *Development Assistance Review, 1981.*
Prebisch, R., 1964, *Towards a New Trade Policy for Development*, report by the Secretary General of UNCTAD, Raul Prebisch, United Nations, New York.
Prebisch, R., 1979, 'La cooperacion internacional en el desarrollo latinoamericano' in *Problemas economicos y sociales de America Latina*. Ediciones Tercer Mundo, Colombia.

Rodriguez, E., 1983, 'Costa Rica en la encrucijada. Analisis de opciones', *Pensamiento Iberoamericano*, No. 4, July/December.

Rohatyn, R., 1983, 'New Bretton Woods conference needed' in 'World Banking', *Financial Times*, 9 May 1983.

Schneider, A., 1980, 'Chile: un analisis critico del desarrollo del sistema financiero', *Economia de America Latina*, No. 4, March.

Seiber, M.J., 1982, *International Borrowing by Developing Countries*, Pergamon Policy Studies in Economic Development, New York: Pergamon Press.

Stewart, F., and A. Sengupta, 1982, *International Financial Cooperation. A Framework for Change*, London: Frances Pinter.

Sunkel, O., 1969, 'External Dependency and National Policy of Development', *Journal of Development Studies*, Vol. 6, No. 1.

UNIDO, 1980, *World Industry since 1960: Progress and Prospects*.

Van Arkadie, B., 1983, 'The IMF Prescription for Structural Adjustment in Tanzania' in Jansen, K., (ed.), *Monetarism, Economic Crisis and the Third World*, London: *Frank Cass*.

World Bank, 1979, *Brazil Human Resources Special Report*, Washington, D.C.

World Bank, 1981, *World Development Report*, Washington, D.C.

World Bank, 1983, *World Development Report*, Washington, D.C.

The International Context for Industrialisation in the Coming Decade

by Raphael Kaplinsky*

Export-orientated industrialisation strategies are currently in vogue, whether as an active choice by LDCs or as a consequence of pressure from the IMF and the World Bank. The attractiveness of these strategies stems from the historic success of the NICs, particularly South Korea, Taiwan, Singapore and Hong Kong. Yet there are signs that the changing nature of the global economy will have a major impact on industrialisation in peripheral economies, and in particular on EOI strategies. This paper focuses on four aspects of this changing international climate – restricted market access, radical electronics-based technical change, the nature of the Structural Adjustment Programmes enforced by the IMF and the World Bank, and the effect of increased military expenditures in the Third World.

I: INTRODUCTION

As Schmitz (in this volume), Kirkpatrick and Nixson [*1983*] and various other observers of the industrialisation process in the Third World have noted, there has been a growing disenchantment with Import Substituting Industrialisation (ISI) and a related acknowledgement of the seeming success over the 1970s of Export-Orientated Industrialisation (EOI) in improving the growth rates of both the manufacturing sectors and the GDPs of the NICs. Not surprisingly, therefore, the prospect of pursuing such outward-orientated development strategies in the coming decade is not without its attractions, both for those countries which had already done so in the past, and for those who had failed to do so. The consequence has been a major reorientating of strategies, both by individual countries[1] and by multilateral agencies.[2]

The task of this paper is to question whether the international context for industrialisation in the coming decade is likely to make such strategies a viable alternative for LDCs.

In questioning the generalisability of the immediate past with the short- to medium-run future, we shall focus on four sets of issues, namely recession and market entry, radical technical change, the effect of the industrial and trade policies enforced by IMF/World Bank Conditionality, and the impact of growing military expenditure on industrial growth. Although they are largely treated as separate issues, there are of course important links

* Institute of Development Studies at the University of Sussex. I am grateful to David Evans, Herbert Schmitz and Sheila Smith for their constructive comments on an earlier draft.

between them. For example the emergence and diffusion of radical new technologies is inextricably linked with the emergence of the global economic crisis and the growth of defence expenditure in the USA [*Kaplinsky, 1984*]. Moreover the discussion must inevitably be bound up with the institutional world – how will MNCs, or Third World states and firms react to the changing trading and economic environment? Most importantly, each of these four sets of issues questions whether the global economic climate in which the NICs achieved their export success over the 1970s will remain structurally unchanged, and in so doing suggests that they are severe obstacles to EOI strategies over the coming decade. It is important to note that we will not be considering in this paper the highly specific *internal* conditions under which EOI proved to be a viable strategy for some LDCs and which inevitably affect the generalisability of the NIC model. (However, see amongst others the contributions by Evans and Alizadeh, and White in this volume.)

II: MARKET ENTRY AND EOI

To begin with, it is essential to recognise the *inherent* limits to the generalisation to other LDCs of the export success of the NICs, the so-called 'fallacy of composition'. Working on the basis of 1976 trade data, Cline [*1982*] calculates that if all LDCs had the same export-intensity as South Korea, Taiwan, Singapore and Hong Kong, adjusting for differences in size and level of industrialisation, this would involve a more-than-700-per cent increase in Third World manufactured exports. *Ceteris paribus* this would increase their share of aggregate DC manufactured imports from 16.7 per cent to 60.4 per cent. Moreover, '... if the product composition is held the same as in the base period, several ... sectors show imports from LDCs in excess of the entire domestic market' [*1982: 85*]. There can be little doubt, therefore, that the pursuit of EOI in the Third World must set itself more modest targets. The issue is the extent of downward revision; the discussion which follows suggests that planners should err on the side of caution rather than optimism.

There is near-unanimity amongst analysts in this field that the key factor facilitating EOI is access to the major markets of the OECD countries. But this unanimity dissolves when it comes to an assessment of the continued likelihood of this market access. Towards the one extreme are Hughes and Waelbroeck [*1981: 144*]: 'For developing countries future prospects seem rather optimistic. Their penetration of industrial-country markets is still low. Room for further penetration exists even in the traditional products, although here penetration and total demand are likely to grow slowly'. Towards the other extreme is Cline's analysis of the fallacy of composition which leads him to conclude that 'It is seriously misleading to hold up the East Asian G-4 (Gang of Four, i.e. Hong Kong, Taiwan, South Korea, Singapore) as a model of development because that model almost certainly cannot be generalised without provoking protectionist response ruling out its implementation' [*1982: 89*]. Our own conclusions tend to align with those of Cline and are based upon the following observations.

To begin with it is important to set the post-World War II expansion of world trade in historical context, for it represented a period of unusually high growth. Tuong and Yeats [*1981*] estimate that whereas global trade expanded at one per cent per annum during 1910–40, the two decades after 1953 saw an annual increase of total trade of eight per cent per annum, and of 11 per cent per annum for manufactures. The consequence was an increasing interdependence of much of the world economy, reflected in part by the share of trade in GDP. In the 1968–78 period alone, the trade:GDP ratio rose from 39 per cent to 48.2 per cent in Germany, from 10.4 per cent to 18 per cent in the USA, 43.7 per cent to 57.3 per cent in the UK, 43.7 per cent to 59.9 per cent in Sweden, and 82.6 per cent to 89.8 per cent for the Netherlands. It hardly needs mentioning that this post-World War II period until the early 1970s was accompanied by reasonably full employment levels in most of the major trading economies.

This expansion of global trade was greatly facilitated by a change in the 'rules' under which exchange occurred, notably a significant reduction in trade barriers. This process was administered over seven rounds by the General Agreement on Trade and Tariffs (GATT). An important component of these various rounds of tariff negotiations was the explicit recognition of the need to offer special assistance to LDCs. In the 1973–79 Tokyo Round, for example, a commitment was made to introducing '... differential measures to developing countries in ways which will provide special and more favourable treatment for them in areas of the negotiation where this was feasible and more appropriate' [*Commonwealth Secretariat, 1982: 29*]. Nevertheless despite this intent, by the end of the Tokyo Round in 1979, the average tariff on 'developing-country type commodities' (7.9 per cent in the nine major developed economies) exceeded that for 'developed country type goods' (i.e. 5.8 per cent) [*ibid: 50*]. Moreover it was noticeable that within the former group, the extent of protection grew with the degree of processing, hence providing obstacles to the deepening of Third World industrialisation, especially that which was resource-based.

However, as the 1970s wore on, the rate of global economic growth declined and unemployment, inflation and balance of payments deficits became endemic in most of the major advanced countries. The rate of growth of world trade – one of the preconditions for EOI strategies in the Third World – also declined, reflecting the slow-down of world economic growth and the increasing incidence of structural rigidities [*UNCTAD, 1983b*]. Trade growth first hiccuped in 1977, and then after a temporary revival fell to 1.5 per cent in 1980, stagnated in 1981 and actually declined in volume (by 2.1 per cent) in 1982. Consequently, despite the evidence that the degree of unemployment caused by imports from LDCs has been marginal[3] and that in aggregate terms the costs of protection exceeded its 'benefits', there has been a growing tendency towards what has come to be called the 'new-protectionism'. Since there was a general commitment to reducing tariff barriers, some other form of entry barrier was required, the result being a plethora of 'non-tariff barriers' (NTBs). These included voluntary export restrictions, orderly marketing arrangements, quotas, preferential government purchasing policies, local content requirements, and subsidies. GATT has recorded over 600 different types of NTBs; UNCTAD recently began to compile an inventory of NTBs, and within two years, had unearthed a record of over 21,000 product-specific measures and an equivalent number of general measures.[4] Moreover, as in the case of tariff measures, NTBs appear to be disproportionately aimed at LDC exports, and escalate as the degree of processing increases [*UNCTAD, 1983a*]. Discussion in international forums now centres around the increasing incidence of NTBs and the lack of 'transparency'[5] in world trade [see also *Diaz-Alejandro and Helleiner, 1982*].

Despite the difficulty of quantifying the significance of this new form of protectionism, it is possible to make a number of observations on their likely incidence in the coming years, all of which lead us to a considerable degree of pessimism with respect to LDCs obtaining the degree of access to DC markets required to justify export-orientated strategies as a primary focus of industrialisation. First we believe that the economic problems now confronting the major economies are likely to last for some years, and that the incidence of protectionism is more likely to grow than decline. There is now substantial evidence (some of it quoted above) that as protectionism increases, LDC exports are relatively worse affected given the weak bargaining power of LDC governments [*Verreydt and Waelbroeck, 1980; UNCTAD, 1983b*]; moreover, the greater the extent of value-added involved, the higher the degree of protection. Second, protectionism appears to be highest in the labour-intensive sectors where LDCs are being advised to specialise on the basis of comparative advantage [*Baldwin, 1970, cited in Helleiner, 1981*]. This is because the *specific* impact of these LDC exports on individual firms, plants, workers and regions producing in developed countries is particularly visible compared to the *generalised* benefits arising from lower-priced consumer goods or expanded LDC purchasing power (see Anderson and Baldwin [*1981*], who summarise a World Bank study of protectionism in 12 developed economies). Third, exports by indigenous Third World firms are likely to be particularly adversely affected by protectionism '... governmental barriers against "disruptive" imports into the North are much more likely when they emanate from firms which are truly "foreign" than when they originate in subsidiaries or affiliates of firms within the importing country' [*Helleiner, 1982a: 55*]. And, finally, associated with this bias against Third World firms' exports, there is the very important issue of whether we are likely to see a continuation of the 1950–75 pattern in which intra-industry trade grew more rapidly than inter-industry trade [*Giersch, 1979*]. Although there are many statistical problems with this analysis on intra-industry trade [*Helleiner, 1981*], at least to some extent it suggests a growing incidence of trade in semi-processed manufactures [*Tharakan, 1979*]. This problem as we will consider further below, is relevant in considering whether we thus can anticipate a relative bias in the incidence of protection against LDC exporters who are not part of the internationalised production network.

This last observation throws the focus of discussion on to the locational decisions of MNCs, who as we saw in earlier sections of this chapter were instrumental both as suppliers and purchasers of LDC manufactured exports in the 1960s and 1970s. The evidence which is now emerging suggests that whatever their past performance (and there are many MNCs who actively seek protective barriers in developed countries), MNCs are being forced to locate production in final markets.[6] This is well illustrated in the case of the colour TV industry [*Ergas, forthcoming*];[7] and is probably but a matter of time in sectors as diverse as steel, automobiles [*Jones and Anderson, 1983*]; electronics [*Rada, 1982a*]; and even perhaps textiles and garments [*Hoffman and Rush, 1983*]. The ability to respond to these protectionist pressures is in part facilitated by the introduction of radical new automation technologies, and it is to this issue that we now turn our attention.

III: RADICAL TECHNICAL CHANGE[8] AND EOI

Despite their antecedents in the late 1940s, the development and diffusion of electronics-based automation technologies was largely a phenomenon of the post-1970 period. It is important to recognise that these radical new technologies are not merely an incremental advance on previous vintages of technical change, since they not only facilitate significant productivity gains, but also involve changes in the systemic organisation of production.

The emergence of these new technologies is best seen in relation to the evolution of previous vintages of automation technology. Initial attempts at mechanisation were concentrated upon the physical *transformation* of materials. Then in the late nineteenth century came the first systematic attempt to automate *handling*, with the emergence of production lines and Taylorist forms of factory organisations. But, although modern *control* devices (the third of the key components of automation technologies, see Bell [*1972*]) date back to the 1930s, it has been the maturation of electronics technologies over the past decade which has given a fillip to the diffusion of automation technologies. The significance of these control techniques lies not just in their low cost, small size, accuracy and rapidity, but also in their common use of binary logic. This allows for the interconnection of electronics devices and throws the emphasis in realising productivity gains on systemic reorganisation [*Halevi, 1982*]. 'The factory of the future' is likely to see not just the increasing automation of physical manufacture, but also the direct linking between manufacture and information co-ordination and design [*Kaplinsky, 1984*].

There are a variety of reasons why the successful utilisation of electronics-based automation technologies benefits innovating firms. First, and despite their software-intensity, fixed *capital* costs are often lowered because they have considerably fewer moving parts and require smaller support structures. More pertinently, because of the greater control facilitated by computerised systems, working capital costs are generally also considerably lower. Second, and most often recognised, is the increased *labour* productivity which arises from their effective use. In computer-aided-design (CAD), for example, the productivity gain has been around 3:1[9] [*Kaplinsky, 1982b*]; in the Japanese automobile industry, the labour content per (X/J sized) vehicle fell from 120-160 hours in 1975 to 95-115 hours in 1980 – moreover '... the effect of robotics is just now beginning to be felt so that labour content in both systems [i.e. Japan and the USA] can be expected to decline considerably in the years ahead' [*Jones and Anderson, 1983: 30*]. Third, due to optimising capabilities, *material* costs can also be significantly cut, both in high technology sectors [*Kaplinsky, 1982b*] and in traditional sectors such as garments [*Hoffman and Rush, 1983*]. Fourth is a reduction in *product development lead-time*, a factor which not just cuts costs but also can be decisive in establishing market shares. The Ford Motor Company, for example, has recently adopted a global 'AJ' (i.e. After Japan) strategy involving the rapid introduction of optimised products – central to this strategy is the rapid adoption of electronics-based automation technologies. And, finally, there is the all-important question of *product quality*. For example, in both the electronic-components and colour TV sectors, the Japanese producers rode to dominance on the backs of higher-quality products – despite initially being more costly. In both cases higher quality was largely dependent upon the use of automated production techniques [*Rada, 1982a and 1982b; Sciberras, 1979*].

There are a number of ways in which the diffusion of these radical, electronics-based automation technologies may affect the viability of EOI strategies in the Third World. In some cases it results from the uneven global diffusion of the technology, but in other respects even if the technology diffuses widely through economic space, there may still be implications for the international location of production, and hence for EOI strategies. But before we turn to the potential impact of these technologies on the international division of labour in manufacturing, it is first useful to examine briefly the likely pattern of the technology's diffusion.

The Diffusion of Electronics-based Automation Technologies

Given the recent emergence of these technologies and the paucity of research in this area we can only generate preliminary conclusions concerning the likely pattern of diffusion. First, on a *sectoral* basis it seems as though the technology is pervasive and will affect most sectors of production, including those traditional manufactures which dominate Third World manufactured exports [*Bessant, 1983*]. Notwithstanding this pervasiveness it would appear as if the technology is diffusing more rapidly to the technology-intensive sectors in which the NICs are hoping to specialise in the future. For example, the sectoral diffusion of CAD technology is directly correlated with the rapidity with which NIC manufactured exports grew over the 1970s [*Kaplinsky, 1982b*]. Second, concerning the *geographical* pattern of diffusion, the evidence, so far is indecisive. Of over 8,000 CAD systems sold by 1980, only 32 went to LDCs [*Kaplinsky, 1982b*]; by contrast Jacobsson [*1982*] estimates that the sectoral turnover/numerically controlled machine tool ratio is higher in South Korea than in Sweden.[10] Leaving aside this evaluation, based on limited evidence, of what *has* actually occurred, it is possible to make some points with regard to *likely* patterns of diffusion on an *a priori* basis. On the positive side the rate of diffusion to LDCs may exceed that to developed countries since the absence of entrenched work practices (by both workers and management) may make it easier to introduce them in greenfield Third World sites than in DCs. With regard to skill-implications, the technology appears to be simple to use, although the effort involved in generating software-based capital goods poses severe pressures in all economies on constrained human resources. On the negative side, though, is the imperative in applications of software-intensive capital goods for users to be close to both other users and vendors; this suggests that there are likely to be economies of agglomeration, at least in the early years of the technologies' diffusion [*Kaplinsky, 1982b and 1984*]. Moreover, as we shall see in later discussion, there is some likelihood that the diffusion of electronics technologies to LDCs is likely to occur selectively in the physical manufacturing sphere of production (rather than in design and information coordination) and this is likely to limit the extent to which the LDCs' enterprises can realise systems gains.

Thus there are reasons to suppose, based at least to some extent on researched evidence, that the technology is diffusing more rapidly to the middle and upper steps of the technological ladder (in which it is crucial that the NICs succeed in order to vacate the lower steps for other LDCs), and more rapidly to developed than developing economies. If this is indeed the case then it is likely that the comparative advantage of Third World producers who do not use the new technology, will be undermined. As a portent for the LDCs it is interesting to consider the case of the colour TV industry in which not only is the automated product of far higher quality, but the labour input in production has fallen so significantly. One of the largest manufacturers estimates that unit construction time has been reduced from 22 hours to one hour over the past decade [*Business week, 1983*]. As the American TV manufacturers have found to their cost, the laggard adoption of new product and process technology in this sector places significant pressures on profits and market shares [*Ergas, forthcoming*]; a similar story can also be told for the automobile industry [*Jones and Anderson, 1983*].

What is interesting is the suggestion that even if the technology diffuses evenly through economic space, the comparative advantage of peripheral Third World producers may nevertheless be undermined. One relevant factor is the impact which a general reduction in the labour output is likely to have in reducing the advantage of low wage costs.[11] Perhaps most striking is the case of the assembly of semi-conductors, one of the major sources of LDC manufactured exports. With the manual technology of the 1970s, Hong Kong production costs were 33 per cent of those in America; with the semi-automatic technology of the early 1980s, the advantage had fallen to 63 per cent; but with automated assembly lines installed in 1983, production costs in Hong Kong were only marginally lower (eight per cent) than those in the US [*Rada, 1984*]. But there are two other ways in which there may be a negative impact on peripheral productions. These are in relation to changing economies of scale, and the emergence of systemo-facture.

Changes in Economies of Scale

In our view one of the major factors explaining the analytical inadequacy of economic theory in relation to the theory of the economies of scale [see

Gold, 1981] arises from its failure to come to terms with the engineering principles which govern these scale economies. Of foremost importance is the distinction between the dimensional and discrete products industry. In the former case there tend to be inherent economies of scale in production.[12] This type of scale economy arises from the process nature of these industries. By contrast in the discrete products industries, scale economies are significantly affected by the downtime involved in resetting machinery specification from one size or type of product to another. Hence in this type of industry, production had tended to bifurcate between dedicated, mass production (e.g. Henry Ford-type assembly lines) and small- or medium-batch production in which differential final demand does not allow for the economies of mass production to be realised. In general the capital goods industries tend to be of a batch production nature – explaining their observed labour intensity [*Stewart, 1978*] – and intermediate and consumer goods industries tend to be mass-production based.[13]

The introduction of the new electronics-based automation technologies is having a profound impact upon these underlying engineering principles affecting scale economies in production, most noticeably in the discrete products industries. This is because their inherent *flexibility* is significantly reducing machine time-settings and their *programmability* is enabling machines to substitute for skilled labour. The consequence is that two opposite effects are emerging. At the mass production end of the spectrum, scale economies are being undermined, whilst at the batch production end, they are being injected [*Ayres and Miller*, 1983]. In both cases, there are substantial implications for the location of industry and hence for the viability of production in peripheral production sites. The reduction of scale economies in the mass production industry is likely to take production closer to the final market and undermine the logic of building 'world plants' and shipping parts around the world.[14] By contrast, the injection of scale economies into batch production is likely to make it difficult for small-scale machinery suppliers, using conventional technology, to compete; this is a problem already facing Southern European firms who are finding domestic and foreign markets being eroded by machinery produced with automated, flexible manufacturing systems.

An additional problem facing LDC producers concerns the distinction between firm-, plant-, and product-economies of scale. Thus whilst the latter two types may be in the process of diminishing (that is, in the mass production industries), firm economies of scale show signs of being enhanced given the higher indirect costs of production associated with the development and utilisation of software-intensive machinery. The evidence available (see Kaplinsky [*1984*] for a summary) suggests that the new technology is diffusing more rapidly to multinational firms even in the developed countries, reflecting in part these firm-economies of scale. If this is the case the relative position of indigenous Third World firms is likely to be undermined.

Systemo-facture

The significant feature of these developments in automation technology is that they place the emphasis in production on systems' economies. The former arises from the mating together of digital-logic control systems within the enterprise. The best known example of this is computer-aided-design/computer-aided-manufacture (CAD/CAM) but even this type of link fails to reflect the advantages being realised in linking together information co-ordination with CAD and CAM. The significance of this point is that unless a firm invests in the new electronics-based automation technology *throughout* the enterprise, and unless the firm also reorganises adequately, then it will be unable to capture the full extent of these systems' gains. In principle, of course, it should be no more difficult for an LDC producer to invest in a full range of automated equipment than in individual items. However, low wage costs make it unlikely that individual sets of machinery will diffuse as rapidly as in DCs.[15] This is likely to be the case particularly in the information processing sphere ('the office'), thereby making it less likely that LDCs firms will be able to take full advantage of intra-firms systems' economies.

Turning to extra-firm systems' economies, the traditional systems under which production occurs is being transformed under the influence of the Japanese. The adoption of the 'last-minute', 'zero-inventory', *Kanban* system enables working capital costs to be cut significantly. (With some components, modern Japanese enterprises work with an inventory of half an hour's production.) However, this form of optimised assembly requires a close link between suppliers and assemblers. In part this explains the recent decision by General Motors to locate component suppliers so close to the final assembly plant, and it is significant that those Japanese firms which have invested in the USA without at the same time ensuring a change in the technology utilised by their component suppliers and in the reorganisation of supply, have not been able to approach the productivity levels realised in Japan [*Schonberger, 1982; Baillie and Felix, 1983; and Hahn et al., 1983*]. Once again this bodes ill for LDC producers, and for two reasons. First, individual automated enterprises are merely one part of systemo-facture. And, second, intra-industry trade (with LDCs providing components, or the labour-intensive parts of components, to DC manufacturers), which as we saw in an earlier section was a major source of trade-growth in the post-war period, is likely to be relatively disadvantaged.

Trade Reversal?

It is still too early to tell how significant – if at all – trade reversal as a result of radical technical change is likely to be. The sector in which the technology has diffused most widely is in the electronics sector itself. Here both Rada [*1982a, 1982b and 1984*] and Ernst [*1982*] have already produced evidence that the assembly of electronics circuits is being brought back from LDCs to DCs, and the introduction of new technologies is likely to further reduce the need for cheap unskilled labour.[16] Similar patterns are evident for the electronics consumer durable industry in which automatic-insertion devices and the utilisation of very large-scale integration (VLSI) components have enabled Japanese TV firms to withdraw from South Korea. Hoffman and Rush [1983] marshall evidence to show that in some sub-processes of the garments industry trade reversal has already occurred and is likely to occur further, and Jones and Anderson [1983] argue that this is also likely to happen in some of those parts of the automobile components sector in which work is presently subcontracted to LDCs. In our view what is clear is that the utilisation of the new technologies will significantly reduce the rate at which production is subcontracted to the Third World; less clear, but probably likely, is a significant degree of trade reversal with subcontracted production being pulled back from low-wage Third World sites.

To summarise this section on radical technical change we began by noting that problems of market entry are forcing producers to locate closer to final markets. The costs of doing so are minimised by the introduction of radical electronics-based automation technologies. This bodes ill for EOI strategies in the Third World, in part because the technology is diffusing unevenly across sectors and economic space, and in part because it has the effect of increasing economies of agglomeration. However, in addition to the twin problems of market access and radical technical change, industrialisation in the Third World is arguably being further threatened by policies introduced at the behest of the IMF and World Bank. It is perhaps ironic that whilst these institutions are amongst the main advocates of EOI, their policies may in fact lead to a significant measure of de-industrialisation, thus undermining the long-run viability of any industrial strategy. It is to these issues which we now turn.

IV: IMF/WORLD BANK CONDITIONALITY AND DE-INDUSTRIALISATION

A discussion of the impact of IMF/World Bank conditionality on de-industrialisation in the Third World treads on stony ground for at least two reasons. First, there is common agreement throughout the ideological spectrum that much of the industrialisation which has occurred in LDCs is difficult to justify on 'efficiency' grounds – however broad the definition of efficiency. In this respect, some de-industrialisation may be a welcome phenomenon, even for those arguing for the extension of industrialisation in the Third World. Second, as Mikesell [1983: 53] points out:

> Since IMF stand-by agreements are secret and the statements regarding their content are limited to generalities, how is it possible for an outsider to evaluate them in terms of the degree of rigour with respect to the nature and comprehensiveness of the policy conditions set forth, the monitoring of performance, or the degree to which conditionality has been enforced?

Despite the problematical nature of this task we believe it is possible to make a brief – albeit tentative – assessment of the impact of these multilateral institutions on the future pattern of industrialisation in the Third World. In order to do so we need to consider the link between industrialisation, debt and conditionality; the linkage between the IMF, the World Bank and the

Commercial Banks; and the types of policies being specified by the IMF and World Bank.

Griffith-Jones and Rodrigues (in this volume) argue that the success of EOI was linked to the growth of Third World debt, although there are obviously variations in the performance of individual economies. One of the major lending institutions throughout the last two decades has been the IMF. But, as Dell points out, 'The method of expanding access [to IMF funds] that has been chosen has the effect of forcing member countries into upper-credit-tranche conditionality much sooner than would occur if quotas had been adjusted appropriately' [1981: 29]. The extent to which LDCs have been forced into this conditionality has consequently increased significantly in recent years – by February 1982 there were standby and Extended Fund Facility (EFF) agreements with 40 LDCs.

Allied to the increasing participation by the Fund in policy-setting in LDCs was the participation by the World Bank with Structural Adjustment loans. By 1982 there had been 12 agreements of this type between the Bank and LDCs [Stern, 1983]. As Dale [1983: 10] observes, 'Because the [IMF] programmes often involve a re-examination of private and public investment policy and of the operations of the public enterprises, the Fund has relied heavily and increasingly on collaboration with the World Bank in helping members assess these programmes.' And linked with the co-ordination of the IMF and the World Bank, is the presence of the Commercial Banking system which after the mid-1970s became an important source of finance for LDCs. In the words of one First Boston Corporation banker [Friedman, 1983: 109]:

> ... commercial banks that do significantly [for them] external lending to developing countries are evolving what is the equivalent of conditionality practised by official national and multinational agencies, that for many borrowing countries this conditionality of private banks is decisively important, and that official borrowers and lenders are increasingly influenced in their own actions by the conditionality of private lenders.

This interlinkage of IMF, World Bank and private bank conditionality is important, so that without the IMF 'seal of approval' it is increasingly unlikely that significant resources will be made available to debtor LDCs. It is instructive therefore to focus on the general orientation of the policies enforced by IMF and World Bank conditionality.[17] Leaving aside the familiar 'composition' problem – that is, if all competing countries devalue simultaneously, the effect is nullified – two elements of conditionality are relevant to the industrialisation of LDCs, namely the 'appropriate' role of the state, and trade and tariff policies.

The Appropriate Role of the State

Traditionally it has been the Fund which has taken a strong line on the appropriate role of the state in LDCs, basing its presumptions on an idealised market-economy model. On many occasions, as in the case of Jamaica (Girvan et al, 1980), a reduction in the role of the state has been an explicit component of IMF conditionality. But in recent years the World Bank has also made a reduction of the role of the state a primary condition for assistance and it is one of the Bank's key policy prescriptions for sub-Saharan Africa. Thus in its recent policy document for the region the 'Berg Report' states 'It is now widely evident that the public sector is over extended, given the present scarcities of financial resources, skilled manpower, and organisational capacity. This has resulted in slower growth than might have been achieved with available resources, and accounts in part for the current crisis' [IBRD, 1982: 5]. Implicit in this is the view that the state is an inefficient allocator of resources, since if this were not the case there would be no point in reducing the relative role of the state in production. The relevance of this to industrial policies is that the history of industrialisation is replete with examples of countries which have industrialised with the state playing an active, interventionist role, not just in policy-setting but also directly in production. Not only is this an historical 'fact' but there are also powerful analytical factors which justify this participation. Notably when external economies exist (arguably the rule, rather than the exception in the early stages of industrialisation) or when there are dynamic learning effects [see Bell, 1982], there is likely to be an under-investment by private capital in industry. Moreover, as Allison and Green [1983] point out, the practical effect of reducing the role of the state may be to increase the role of foreign capital. As we argued above, in the changing economic climate of the 1980s, we believe that foreign investors will be increasingly reluctant to use LDCs as production platforms for the world market.

Trade and Tariff Policies

The multilateral agency position on trade and tariff policies is heavily conditioned by the apparent link between protection and 'inefficiency' (that is, the extent of value-added in world prices) on the one hand, and that between 'free trade' policies and export success on the other. At various places in this volume the causality implicit in this linkage has been questioned, and so has the accuracy of the assertion that 'free trade-type' conditions have prevailed in those economies such as South Korea and Taiwan, which are often held up as models for other LDCs. In this discussion we will focus briefly on the conception of indigenous technical capability implicit in the trade policies pursued by the Bank and the IMF, and its effects on long-run industrial expansion.

The problem here is that because of the confidentiality involved in conditionality agreements it is difficult to provide chapter and verse verification of the policies which have been pursued.[18] Even Balassa, seemingly influential in World Bank policy formation over the years, whilst suggesting that rates of effective protection should not exceed 10 per cent, and that specific infant industry protection should not exceed 'five to eight years' [Balassa, 1982: 69], is imprecise over the time period involved in reaching the optimal levels. 'This level [i.e. 10 per cent effective protection] may be considered a long-term target, to be reached over time.'[19] Yet, few observers would demur at the conclusion that the consistent drift of this policy has been to reduce protection significantly within reasonably short (five to eight years) periods of time. Such prescriptions reveal a general lack of historical analysis. For both at the macro- and sector-specific level, EOI was generally preceded by industrial experience accumulated over many decades. Thus, whilst much of the ISI in current LDCs may appear to be 'inefficient' and ephemeral, it may well be an important investment in the long run. Consider, for example, the case of sugar technology [*Kaplinsky, 1983a*]. Here the development of the dominant vacuum-pan technology took around 100 years (1820–1920); beet sugar technology matured over a period of 50 heavily protected years (1800–1850) and the Indian development of open-pan technology (which has recently 'matured' and become competitive) took around 50 years (1925–1980). Bell [*1982*] in his recent review of infant industries, identifies similarly long-time horizons in the case of DCs and LDCs alike. But the sort of time-framework implicit in the Bank/Fund conditionality is considerably shorter and in our view this has a very important implication for technical 'mastery', technical change and technological capability. We conclude that the shorter time-periods may be ideally suited to importing technology from abroad and rooting out X-inefficiency, but have little relevance to developing some form of indigenous capability or technological 'mastery', which takes a much greater period of time and is arguably a precondition for sustained, long-run industrialisation.

These observations should not be taken as a blanket support for protection. For not only is it transparently obvious that some industrialisation in the Third World is difficult to justify whatever the conception of 'efficiency',[20] but as Bell [*1982*] points out, protection is by no means a sufficient condition for indigenous technological change. Rather, the point we wish to make here is that the form in which conditionality has actually been implemented is, despite some protestations to the contrary, blunt, and that the general effect is to enforce de-industrialisation on the Third World. By doing so it not only lets the dirty water out of the bath but forces the screaming baby through the plug-hole at the same time.

To sum up this section on conditionality and de-industrialisation, therefore, we would refer to the brief and restrained comments of Helleiner on the relevance of these criteria for policy information which, we have argued, may in some cases enforce de-industrialisation in a highly unselective manner:

> . . . while liberal policies are part of IMF and World Bank wisdom, there exist examples of rapid growth achieved with an interventionist state, and the benefits and costs of protectionism are quite widely perceived as varying with the size of country, the level of development, and other factors. The cost of transition to a more liberal trade or payments regime can be calculated and compared with the possible benefits in particular circumstances; it may be quite rational for policy workers who sincerely prefer liberal policies to hesitate before incurring the costs of taking the first steps in that general direction [*Helleiner, 1983: 581*].

V: MILITARY EXPENDITURES AND INDUSTRIALISATION

As Smith and Smith [*1983*] point out, the precise content of many of the numbers used to argue that military expenditure is either functional or disfunctional to industrial growth is open to question.[21] It is difficult therefore to determine the direction of the overall share of global GDP spent on the military sector. Despite this ambiguity the sums involved are staggering. World military expenditure in 1980 (between $510 billion and $630 billion) was 15-20 times more than total official Development Aid; even in the 1960s (a period of *détente*), total global military expenditure grew at a real rate of 1.8 per cent per annum and more recently in the late 1970s, this rose to three per cent per annum; 50 million people are employed in the military sector globally (of whom half are soldiers); more significantly for this discussion:

> It is in the field of science and technology, however, that the diversion of resources to military ends is greatest. Recent estimates indicate that up to 20-25 per cent of the world's scientific and research activities are directed towards military purposes. The research intensity of the average military product is some 20 times higher than that of an average non-military manufactured product [*UNCTAD, 1982a: 204*].

Finally one of the more striking features of the changing pattern of military expenditure is the increasing share by the Third World. This rose from around 20 per cent of the total in 1950 to around 30 per cent in 1980.

The link between this military expenditure and industrial growth is a subject of some debate. Some macro-economic studies, beginning from the observation that the most rapidly growing OECD economies in the post-war period (Japan and Germany) were those with the smallest military/GDP ratios, have tended to argue that these expenditures have a high opportunity cost [*Smith and Smith, 1983; Smith and Georgiou, 1983*]. This has been confirmed by various sectoral studies in the UK [*Pavitt, 1981*] which have illustrated how high military expenditures are associated with a reduction in international competitiveness, a view confirmed recently by the former Chief UK Government scientist's report on the lack of spillover from high military expenditures to the civilian sector [*NEDO, 1983*]. In contrast it is possible to show a fairly high degree of spin-off from the military sector to automation technology in the US, but difficult to determine the opportunity costs of these military outlays [*Kaplinsky, 1984*]. In general, however, there is fairly widespread recognition that in the advanced economies military expenditures have a high opportunity cost and tend to undermine the international competitiveness of industrial sectors.

By extension we can anticipate on an *a priori* basis a similar relationship with respect to LDCs. This is graphically illustrated in the Indian Ocean region. Here changes in the US submarine-based missile technology have moved the arena of conflict from the Arabian Gulf to the equatorial zone [*Kaplinsky, 1983b*] and at the same time the need to maintain oil supplies has led to the build-up of the US Rapid Deployment forces in the area. This is having a major consequence for all the surrounding economies, and in particular for India. Faced with the delivery of sophisticated F–16 planes to a potentially nuclear-powered adversary, Indian industrial strategy is being significantly affected, such that increasing dependence is being placed upon foreign technology and inappropriate industries [Lal, 1982].[22] This increasing militarisation of the Indian Ocean region is coincident with an invasion of the Comoros and Seychelles Islands, military governments in Pakistan, Sudan, Ethiopia and Somalia and an attempted coup in Kenya. It is also associated with an increasing diversion of foreign exchange, investment and human skills from other sectors (including industry) thereby reducing the viability of industrial strategies in the region.

It is not merely the aggregate size and opportunity cost of military expenditure which threatens to undermine the viability of industrial strategies in the Third World, but also the nature of the technologies which are utilised. For example, a squadron of F–11 Phantom aircraft requires an inventory of around 70,000 spares, with extensive additional infrastructural support. These weapons systems grow increasingly complex,[23] drawing further upon constrained human and technical resources, demanding large-scale support systems and, as a consequence, having low levels of reliability. Sophisticated, import- and capital-equipment is essential to maintain the equipment and the result is a complex enclave (both in the social and economic senses) of military-related activities.

The impact of these developments on the Third World is not clear-cut however. As in the early industrial histories of the advanced economies [Kaldor, 1981] it is at least possible that in some circumstances high levels of military expenditure can facilitate industrial growth by upgrading the level of technological capability in the economy. This is at least a working hypothesis for countries such as South Africa (relatively free of balance of payments constraints), Israel and Brazil. Yet despite the possibility of individual economies being exceptions to a general tendency, the evidence suggests four major conclusions relevant to the future of industrial strategies in the Third World. (Constrained space prohibits us from more detailed treatment of these issues.) First, in general, military expenditure tends to displace scarce resources (especially human skills and foreign exchange) from the industrial sector. Second, these military expenditures are often associated with military rule in which the military apparatus assumes a parasitic rather than a progressive role. Third, the social and economic nature of military enclaves in the Third World imposes a series of structures which are highly inappropriate to the requirements for sustained industrial growth. And, finally, the onset of the new cold war is accompanied by an increasing globalisation of the geo-strategic stand-off, with renewed militarisation in Central America, and the onset of a regional arms race in the heavily populated Indian Ocean region. From the standpoint of industrial growth in large parts of the Third World over the coming years, the picture looks distinctly gloomy.

VI: CONCLUSIONS

It would be a mistake to overdramatise the significance of the points under discussion in this paper. Whilst clearly particularly relevant to the viability of the EOI strategies which are currently being dangled in front of LDC governments and enterprises, the four issues treated in this paper will not by themselves make EOI a phenomenom of the past. There will no doubt still be space for some measure of outward-orientated industrialisation (particularly, in our view, that which involves greater intra-Third World trade) and indeed there is some evidence that an embryonic second tier of new-NICs may have begun to emerge [*Havrylyshyn and Alikhani, 1982*]. Yet to swing from this caveat to the export optimism implicit in most Structural Adjustment programmes would in our view be even more mistaken. There can be no doubt that we are witnessing major changes in manufacturing technology which threaten to change the economics of location and that market entry is becoming an increasingly severe problem for many Third World exporters. At the same time the content of Structural Adjustment programmes, by undermining the pervasive role of the state and focusing on short-run static efficiency is placing significant obstacles in the face of long-run industrial strategies. Finally, and perhaps most depressingly, we appear to be moving into an increasingly militarised era, such that many peripheral economies are being drawn into the conflict between the superpowers, resulting not only in costly and inappropriate military expenditure, but also in patterns of social relations which are inimical to sustained industrialisation and development.

NOTES

1. Most LDCs, including China, have now explicitly chosen such growth strategies. One indication of this is to be seen in the establishment of Export Processing Zones which increased in number from about 220 to over 350 between 1978 and 1980.
2. Witness the recent World Bank strategy document for Africa [*IBRD, 1982*].
3. See, for example, Verreydt and Waelbroeck [*1980*]; Anderson and Baldwin [*1981*] and UNCTAD [*1983b*].
4. Unfortunately the recent origins of the UNCTAD data bank, as well as the very nature of the NTBs in question, make it difficult to 'prove' that NTBs are on the increase. However, few doubt this to be the case.
5. As the UNCTAD document notes, in April 1982 the EEC alone published 138 Import Regulations making it difficult for enterprises to keep abreast of changes in the trading environment.
6. In the words of one of the leaders of the US Auto Workers Union, the Japanese car producers 'should put their plants where their markets are'.
7. It is significant that in recent years a Taiwanese TV firm has taken over a British company to gain entry into Europe; the Koreans have set-up a TV subsidiary in the USA; and a Brazilian firm has taken over a hi-fi manufacturer in the UK. All have occurred to counter protectionist measures.
8. Many of the points made in this section are drawn from Kaplinsky [*1984*].
9. It is noteworthy, however, that when asked to rank the significance of the new technology, most users put product improvements and reduced product lead-time ahead of labour productivity gains [*Kaplinsky, 1982b; Arnold and Senker, 1982*].
10. However, no account is taken of value-added or of the complexity of the NC machine tools involved, which makes it difficult to reach determinate conclusions; moreover, country

comparisons are for different time-periods, thereby overemphasising the relative performance of South Korea.

11. Another example is that despite price rises of Japanese automobiles, and despite wage increases, unit labour costs of Japanese J/X sized cars remained constant between 1975 and 1980 [*Jones and Anderson, 1983*].

12. As in the chemical industry's 'six-tenths rule' [*Chilton, 1960*], which states that the relationship between cost and scale is similar to that between surface area and volume.

13. It is significant that the 'traditional manufactures' – notably garment and leather products – tend to be of a batch and low-technology nature, and hence (unskilled) labour-intensive, thereby largely accounting for the dominance of Third World production in these sectors.

14. For example, in the 1970s General Motors set up three engine assembly plants in Austria, Australia and Brazil to meet its global needs for a new engine; its 1980s strategy for the USA [*Gooding, 1983*] is to have all component suppliers within 100 miles radius of its final assembly plant.

15. For example, going back to CAD equipment, in many LDCs gross annual wage costs are higher than $8,000, which in 1980 prices was the switchover point at which CAD became the preferred, cost cutting technology [*Kaplinsky, 1982b*].

16. Such as the 'surface mounting' of integrated circuits which avoids the necessity to encase them in plastic packages and fix connectors, tasks traditionally done by cheap labour in LDCs [*Financial Times, 1983*].

17. General descriptions of World Bank Structural Adjustment Program support is given for eight countries in Landell-Mills, [*1981*], and for 12 countries in Stern [*1983*].

18. For example, in Stern's table on World Bank Structural Adjustments Loans [*1983: 94*] individual agreements are specified in terms of whether they cover: (i) Exchange rate policy; (ii) Tariff reform and import liberalisation; and (iii) Export incentives and improved institutional support.

19. This statement is footnoted 'Lower target rates may be appropriate in semi-industrial developing countries in which the share of manufacturing in the gross national product approaches that in developed countries'.

20. One of the more extreme cases known to the author was the suggestion by EEC consultants that one small African island-economy assemble motor cars. Total annual sales of all vehicles in the economy was less than 500!

21. For example, the CIA calculations of the cost of the Soviet armaments programme is based upon assessing real numbers of personnel and equipment and then grossing them up to a dollar value, based on US costs. Thus inflation in American equipment prices, or a rise in salaries in the US annual forces, is reflected in an increase in the size of the Soviet arms budget and in its share of GDP!

22. Lal is a former Air Chief Marshal of the Indian Air Force.

23. 'The pressure this puts on the budget has been neatly illustrated by a calculation which showed that, based on a simple extrapolation of long-lasting trends, by the year 2036 the entire US military budget would be able to afford but a single combat aircraft'! [*Smith and Smith 1983: 34*].

REFERENCES

Abernathy, W.J., 1978, *The Productivity Dilemma: Roadblock to Innovation in the Automobile Industry*, Baltimore and London: Johns Hopkins University Press.

Albrecht, U. and M. Kaldor (eds.), 1979, *The World Military Order*, London: Macmillan.

Allison, C. and R. Green (eds.), 1983, 'Accelerated Development in Sub-Saharan Africa', *Bulletin of the Institute of Development Studies*, Vol. 14, No. 1, Brighton: University of Sussex.

Anderson, K. and R.E. Baldwin, 1981, 'The Political Market for Protection in Industrial Countries: Empirical Evidence', *World Bank Staff Working Paper*, No. 492, Washington D.C.: International Bank for Reconstruction and Development.

Arnold, E. and P. Senker, 1982, Designing the Future: The Implications of CAD Interactive Graphics for Employment and Skills in the British Engineering Industry, *Occasional Paper*,

No. 9, Watford: Engineering Industries Training Board.

ARTEP, 1981, 'The General Trading Companies of Japan and Export-led Industrialisation', in G. Lee (ed.) [*1981*].

Ayres, R.U. and S. Miller, 'Robotics, CAM and Industrial Productivity', *National Productivity Review*, Vol. 1, No. 1, pp. 452-60.

Baillie, A.S. and D. Felix, 1973, 'Kanban: A Fundamental Solution to Production Problems', paper presented at the Second United States–Japan Business Conference, Tokyo, 5 April.

Bairoch, P., 1975, *The Economic Development of the Third World Since 1900*, London: Methuen.

Balassa, B., 1980, The Process of Industrial Development and Alternative Development Strategies, *World Bank Staff Working Paper*, No. 438, Washington, D.C.: International Bank for Reconstruction and Development.

Balassa, B., 1982, 'Reforming the System of Incentives in Developing Economies', in B. Balassa and Associates, *Development Strategies in Semi-industrial Economies*, Baltimore: Johns Hopkins University Press.

Balassa, B., 1983, 'The Adjustment Experience of Developing Economies after 1973', in J. Williamson (ed.) [*1983: 145-74*].

Baldwin, R.E., 1970, *Non-tariff Distortions in International Trade*, Washington: Brookings Institution.

Bell, R.M., 1972, *Changing Technology and Manpower Requirements in the Engineering Industry*, Brighton: University of Sussex.

Bell, R.M., 1982, 'Technological Change in Infant Industries: A Review of Empirical Evidence', mimeo, Science Policy Research Unit, University of Sussex.

Bessant, J., 1983, *Microprocessors in Production Processes*: London: Policy Studies Institute.

Bienefeld, M. and M. Godfrey (eds.), 1982, *The Struggle for Development: National Strategies in an International Context*, Chichester: J. Wiley & Sons.

Business Week, 1983, 'Philips' High-Tech Crusade', 18 July, pp. 96-103.

Chilton, C.H. (ed.), 1960, *Cost Engineering in the Process Industries*, New York: McGraw-Hill.

Cline, W.R., 1982, 'Can the East Asian Model of Development be Generalized?', *World Development*, Vol. 10, No. 2, pp. 81-90.

Commonwealth Secretariat, 1982, *Protectionism: Threat to International Order: The Impact on Developing Countries*, London: Report by a Group of Experts.

Dale, W.B., 1983, 'Financing and Adjustments of Payments Imbalances', in J. Williamson (ed.) [*1983: 3-16*].

Datta-Chaudhuri, M.K., 1981, 'Industrialisation and Foreign Trade: The Development Experiences of South Korea and the Philippines', in G. Lee (ed.) [*1981*].

Dell, S., 1981, 'On being grandmotherly: the evolution of IMF conditionality', *Princeton University Essays in International Finance*, No. 144, New Jersey.

Dell, S., C. Diaz-Alejandro, R. French-Davis, T. Gudac, C. Ossa, 1981, 'Studies on International Monetary and Financial Issues for the Developing Countries' Structural Adjustment Policies', New York, *UNDP/Unctad Project Report to the Group of Twenty Four, UNCTAD/MED/TA/15*.

Diaz-Alejandro, C.F. and G.K. Helleiner, 1982, *Handmaiden in Distress: World Trade in the 1980s*, Ottawa: North–South Institute.

Edgren, G., 1982, 'Spearheads of Industrialisation or Sweatshops in the Sun?: A Critical Appraisal of Labour Conditions in Asian Export Processing Zones', Bangkok: ILO–ARTEP Working Paper.

Einzig, P., 1957, *The Economic Consequences of Automation*, London: Secker and Warburg.

Electronic Industries Association of Korea, 1982 *Electronics Industry in Korea*, Seoul.

Ergas, H., forthcoming, 'Restricting Japan – Who Benefits?', *The World Economy*.

Ernst, D., 1982, *The Global Race in Microelectronics: Innovation and Corporate Strategies in a Period of Crisis*, Frankfurt: Campus.

Financial Times, 1983, 'Fixing Electronic Components on to Printed Circuit Boards', 17 February.

Forester, T. (ed.), 1980, *The Microelectronics Revolution*, Oxford: Basil Blackwell.

Fransman, M. and K. King (eds.), 1984, *Technological Capability in the Third World*, London: Macmillan.

Friedman, I.S., 1983, 'Private Bank Conditionality: Comparison with the IMF and the World Bank', in J. Williamson (ed.) [*1983: 109-28*].

Georgiou, G., 1983, 'The Political Economy of Military Expenditure'. *Capital and Class*, No. 19, Spring, pp. 183-204.

Giersch, H. (ed.), 1979, *On the Economies of Intra-Industry Trade*, Tubingen: J.C.R. Mohr.

Gillies, G.I., 1983, '*International Production and Trade: The Case for Focusing on their Complementarity*', paper presented at the Annual Conference of the Academy of International Business, University of Strathclyde, Glasgow.

Girvan, N., R. Bernal., W. Hughes, 1980, 'The IMF and the Third World: The Case of Jamaica, 1974–80', *Development Dialogue*, No. 2, pp. 113-55.

Godfrey, M., 1983, 'Export Orientation and Structural Adjustment in Sub-Saharan Africa', in C. Allison and R. Green (eds.) [*1983: 39-44*].

Gold, B., 1981, 'Changing Perspectives on Size, Scale and Returns: An Interpretive Survey', *Journal of Economic Literature*, Vol. XIX, March, pp. 5-33.

Gooding, K., 1983, 'Assemblers' Dilemma', *Financial Times*, 26 May (Vehicle Components III).

Griffith-Jones, S. and D. Seers (eds.), 1981, *Monetarism and The Third World*, Bulletin of the Institute of Development Studies, Vol. 13, No. 1.

Hahn, C.K., P.A. Pinto., D.J. Bragg, 1983, 'MRP vs KANBAN – New Perspectives in Production and Inventory Control', paper presented at the Second United States–Japan Business Conference, Tokyo, 5 April.

Halevi, G., 1982, *The Role of Computers in Manufacturing Processes*, Chichester: John Wiley & Sons.

Havrylyshyn, O. and L. Alikhani, 1982, 'Is There Cause for Export Optimism? An Inquiry into the Existence of a Second Generation of Successful Exporters', *Weltwirschaftliches Archive*, Vol. 118, No. 4, pp. 651-63.

Havrylyshyn, O., and M. Wolf, 1982, 'Promoting Trade Among Developing Countries: An Assessment', *Finance and Development*, Vol. 19, No. 1.

Helleiner, G.K. (ed.), 1981, *Intra-Firm Trade and the Developing Countries*, London: Macmillan.

Helleiner, G.K. (ed.), 1982a, *For Good or Evil: Economic Theory and North–South Negotiations*, Toronto: University of Toronto Press.

Helleiner, G.K., 1982b, '*International Trade Theory and Northern Protectionism against Southern Manufacture*', in G.K. Heilleiner [*1982a*].

Helleiner, G.K., 1983, '*Panel Discussion*', in J. Williamson (ed.) [*1983*].

Hoffman, K. and R. Rush, 1982, *Microelectronics and the Garment Industry: 'not yet a perfect fit'*, in R. Kaplinsky (ed.) [*1982a*].

Hoffman, K. and R. Rush, 1983, *Microelectronics and Clothing: The Impact of Technical Change on a Global Industry*, Geneva: ILO.

Hone, A., 'Multinational Corporations and Multinational Buying Groups: Their Impact on the Growth of Asian Exports of Manufactures – Myths and Realities', *World Development*, Vol. 2, No. 2.

Hsia, R., 1979, 'Technological Change, Trade Promotion and Export-Led Industrialization (with reference to Hong Kong and South Korea)', *ILO Asian Employment Programme Working Paper II-2*, Bangkok. Also reprinted in E. Lee (ed.) [*1981*].

Hughes, H. and J. Waelbroeck, 1981, 'Can Developing-country Exports Keep Growing in the 1980s?', *The World Economy*, Vol. 4, No. 2, June, pp. 127-48.

Institut Francais des Relations Internationales, 1982, *Ramses 1982: The State of the World Economy*, London: Macmillan.

International Bank for Reconstruction and Development (IBRD), 1982, *World Development Report*, Washington: Oxford University Press/IBRD.

International Labour Office, Asian Employment Programme, 1980, *Export-Led Industrialisation and Employment: Proceedings of a Symposium*, Geneva: ILO.

International Monetary Fund, *Surveys*.

International Monetary Fund/International Bank for Reconstruction and Development, *Finance and Development*.

Jacobsson, S., 1981, 'Technical Change and Technology Policy: The Case of Numerically Controlled Lathes in Argentina', mimeo, Lund, Sweden.

Jacobsson, S., 1982, 'Electronics and the Technology Gap – the Case of Numerically Control-
led Machine Tools', in R. Kaplinsky (ed.) [1982a: 42-6].
Jacobsson, S. and J. Sigurdson (eds.), 1983, *Technological Trends and Challenges in Electro-
nics: Dominance of the Industrial World and Responses in the Third World*, Research Policy
Institute, University of Lund.
Jones, D. and M. Anderson, 1983, 'Competition in the World Auto Industry: Implications for
Production Location', mimeo, University of Sussex.
Jones, D.T., 1983, 'Technology and Employment in the UK Automobile Industry', mimeo,
Science Policy Research Unit, University of Sussex.
Jose, N.R., 1982, *Mortgaging the Future: The World Bank and IMF in the Philippines*, Quezon
City: Foundation for Nationalist Studies.
Kaldor, M., 1981, *The Baroque Arsenal*, London: Andre Deutsch.
Kaplinsky, R., 1982a (ed.), 'Comparative Advantage in an Automating World', *Bulletin of the
Institute of Development Studies*, Vol. 13, No. 2, Institute of Development Studies, Uni-
versity of Sussex, Brighton.
Kaplinsky, R., 1982b, *Computer Aided Design: Electronics, Comparative Advantage and
Development*, London: Frances Pinter.
Kaplinsky, R., 1982c, 'Fractions of Capital and Accumulation in Kenya', mimeo, Institute of
Development Studies, University of Sussex, Brighton.
Kaplinsky, R., 1983a, *Sugar Processing: The Development of a Third World Technology*,
London: Intermediate Technology Publishers.
Kaplinsky, R., 1983b, 'Accumulation at the Periphery: A Special Case?' in R. Cohen (ed.),
African Islands and Enclaves, 1983, Beverley Hills and London: Sage.
Kaplinsky, R., 1983c, 'Trade in Technology, Who, What, Where and When?', in M. Fransman
and K. King (eds.) [*1984*].
Kaplinsky, R., 1984, *Automation: The Technology and Society*, London: Longmans.
Killick, T., 1981a, 'IMF Stabilisation Programmes', *ODI Working Paper*, No. 6, London:
Overseas Development Institute.
Kirkpatrick, C.H. and F.I. Nixson (eds.), *The Industrialisation of Less Developed Countries*,
Manchester: Manchester University Press.
Lal, P.C., 1982, 'US Arms for Pakistan', *Seminar*, February, pp. 21-5.
Landell-Mills, P.M., 1981. 'Structural adjustment lending: early experience', *Finance and
Development*, Vol. 18, No. 4, December, pp. 7-21.
Lee, E. (ed.), 1981, *Export-led Industrialisation and Development*, Geneva: ILO.
Little, I.M.B., 1979, 'The Experience and Causes of Rapid Labour-Intensive Development in
Korea, Taiwan, Hong Kong and Singapore, and the Possibilities of Emulation *ILO Asian
Employment Programme Working Paper* II-1, Bangkok: International Labour Office, also
reprinted in E. Lee (ed.) [*1981*].
Mikesell, R.F., 1983, 'Appraising IMF Conditionality: Too Loose, Too Tight, or Just Right?',
in J. Williamson (ed.) [*1983: 47-62*].
NEDO, 1983, *The Commercial Exploitation of Defence Technology*, London: National Econo-
mic Development Office.
Northcott, A. with P. Rogers and A. Zeilinger, 1981a, *Microelectronics in Industry: Extent of
Use*, London: Policy Studies Institute.
Northcott, J. with P. Rogers and A. Zeilinger, 1981b, *Microelectronics in Industry: Advantages
and Problems*, London: Policy Studies Institute.
Northcott, J., 1982, *Microelectronics in Industry: What's Happening in Britain*, London: Policy
Studies Institute.
Noyce, R., 1977, 'Microelectronics', *Scientific American*, September, reprinted in T. Forester
(ed.) [*1980: 29-41*].
Paauw, D.S., 1979, 'Frustrated Labour-Intensive Development: The Case of Indonesia', *ILO
Asian Employment Programme Working Paper*, II-3, Bangkok, also reprinted in G. Lee
(ed.) [*1981*].
Pavitt, K. (ed.), 1981, *Technical Innovation and British Economic Performance*, London:
Macmillan.
Pirenne, H., 1961, *Economic and Social History of Medieval Europe*, London: Routledge &
Kegan Paul.
Plesch, P.A., 1978, *Developing Countries' Exports of Electronics and Electrical Engineering*

Products, Washington, D.C.: International Bank for Reconstruction and Development, Economics of Industry Division.

Pratten, C.F., 1971, *Economies of Scale in Manufacturing*, Cambridge: Cambridge University Press.

Rada, J., 1980, *The Impact of Micro-Electronics*, Geneva: ILO.

Rada, J., 1982a, *Structure and Behaviour of the Semiconductor Industry*, paper prepared for the United Nations Center on Transnationals, mimeo, Geneva.

Rada, J., 1982b, 'Technology and the North–South division of labour' in R. Kaplinsky (ed.) [*1982a: 5-13*].

Rada, J., 1984, *International Division of Labour and Technology*, Geneva: ILO.

Sampson, G.P., 1980, 'Contemporary Protectionism and Exports of Developing Countries', *World Development*, February.

Schonberger, R.J., 1982, *Japanese Manufacturing Techniques: Nine Hidden Lessons in Simplicity*, New York: The Free Press.

Sciberras, R., 1979, 'Technology Transfer to Developing Countries – Implications for Member Countries' Science and Technology Policy', *Television and Related Products Sector Final Report*, Paris: OECD.

Silberston, A., 1972, 'Economies of Scale in Theory and Practice', *Economic Journal*, March 1972, pp. 369-91. (Reprinted in L. Wagner and N. Baltazzis (eds.), 1973, *Readings in Applied Microelectronics*, Oxford: Clarendon Press.)

Singh, A., 1983, 'Third World Industrialisation: Industrial Strategies and Policies in the 1980s and 1990s', mimeo, Faculty of Economics, University of Cambridge.

Sivard, R.L., annual, *World Military and Social Expenditure*.

Smith, D. and R. Smith, 1983, *The Economics of Militarism*, London: Pluto Press.

Smith, R. and G. Georgiou, 1983, 'Assessing the Effect of Military Expenditure on OECD Economies: A Survey', mimeo, Economics Department, Birkbeck College, London.

Stern, E., 1983, 'World Bank Financing of Structural Adjustment', in J. Williamson (ed.) [*1983: 87-107*].

Stewart, F., 1978, *Technology and Underdevelopment*, London: Macmillan.

Swords-Isherwood, N., and P. Senker, 1980, *Microelectronics and the Engineering Industry: The Need for Skills*, London: Frances Pinter.

Tharakan, P.K.M., 1979, 'A Survey of Alternative Views' in European Centre for Study of Information on Multinational Corporations, *The International Division of Labour and Multinational Companies*, Farnborough: Saxon House.

Tuomi, H. and R. Vayryuen, 1982, *Transnational Corporations, Armaments and Development*, New York: St. Martin's Press.

Tuong Ho Dac and A.J. Yeats, 1981, 'Market Disruption, the New Protectionism, and Developing Countries: A Note on Empirical Evidence from the US', *The Developing Economies*, Vol. XIX, No. 2, June, pp. 107-18.

Tzong-biau, Lin and V. Mark, 1980, *Trade Barriers and the Promotion of Hong Kong's Exports*, Hong Kong: Chinese University Press.

United Nations, 1981, 'Transnational Corporations and Transborder Data Flows: An Overview', UN Economic and Social Council, Commission on Transnational Corporations, E/C. 10/87, New York.

United Nations Centre on Transnational Corporations, 1982, 'Transnational Corporations in the International Auto Industry', ST/CTC/38, New York.

United Nations Conference on Trade and Development (UNCTAD), 1979, 'The industrial policies of the developed market economy countries and the effect on the exports of manufactures and semi-manufactures from the developing countries', TD/230/Supp 1/Rev 1, New York: United Nations.

United Nations Conference on Trade and Development, 1980, 'Trade in Manufacture of Developing Countries and Territories: 1977', TD/B/C.2/187, New York: United Nations.

United Nations Conference on Trade and Development, 1981, *Trade and Development Report*, TD/B/863/Rev 1, New York: United Nations.

United Nations Conference on Trade and Development, 1982a, *Trade and Development Report*, ITDR/2, Geneva: United Nations.

United Nations Conference for Trade and Development, 1982b, 'Incentives for Industrial Exports', TD/B/C.2/184, New York: United Nations.

United Nations Conference on Trade and Development, 1982c, 'The Impact of Electronics Technology on the Capital Goods and Industrial Machinery Sector: Implications for Developing Countries', TD/B/C.6/Ac.7/3, Geneva: United Nations.

United Nations Conference on Trade and Development, 1983a, 'Non-tariff Barriers Affecting the Trade of Developing Countries and Transparency in World Trading Conditions: the Inventory of Non-tariff Barriers', TD/B/940, Geneva: United Nations.

United Nations Conference on Trade and Development, 1983b, 'Protectionism and Structural Adjustment: An Overview', TD/B/942, Geneva: United Nations.

United Nations Development Programme/United Nations Conference on Trade and Development, 1979, *The Balance of Payments Adjustment Process in Developing Countries*, New York: United Nations.

Verreydt, E. and J. Waelbroeck, 1980, 'European Community Protection against Manufactured Imports from Developing Countries', *World Bank Staff Working Paper*, No. 432, Washington, D.C.: International Bank for Reconstruction and Development.

Westphal, L., Y.W. Rhee, G. Pursell, 1981, 'Korean Industrial Competence: Where it Came From', *World Bank Staff Working Paper*, No. 469, Washington, D.C.: International Bank for Reconstruction and Development.

Williamson, J., 1982b, 'The Economics of IMF Conditionality', in G.K. Helleiner [*1982a*].

Williamson, J., (ed.), 1983, *IMF Conditionality*, Institute for International Economics, Cambridge, Mass.: Massachusetts Institute of Technology Press.

Developmental States and Socialist Industrialisation in the Third World

*by Gordon White**

Development Economics as a discipline and the idea of the state as the organiser of economic activity are inseparable. Basic concepts and distinctions are put forward to unravel the complex question of the role of the state in the industrialisation process. These are then used to examine the state in three waves of socialist industrialisation which shows a strong capacity to mobilise and direct economic, social and political resources. The typically pervasive state may, however, outlive its historically progressive role and become a bastion of economic irrationality and political authoritarianism.

I: THE DEVELOPMENTAL STATE

The modern notion of 'development', and not least the discipline of 'development economics', rests on a more or less explicit concept of the state as crucial stimulant and organiser of socio-economic progress. This intellectual paradigm has drawn historical sustenance from the argument [especially *Gerschenkron, 1966*] that successful 'late development' takes a form very different from that of earlier industrialisers, notably the United Kingdom. The developmental process is less 'spontaneous', more subject to teleological determination, with the state as a major agent of social transformation in both capitalist (Japan, Germany) and socialist (Soviet Union) contexts. Modern conceptions of 'development' were also heavily influenced both by the rise of the social democratic welfare state and Keynesian 'managerial state' in Western industrialised countries and the experience of successful planned industrialisation in the Soviet bloc.

The ideology of 'developmentalism' and the idea of the interventionist state are inseparable. Over the past three decades, development analysts and policy-makers have, implicitly or explicitly, viewed the state as the primary mechanism for overcoming certain major constraints inherent in the domestic and international context of the 'new nations'. (For good reviews, see Green [*1974*] and Murray [*1975*].) Where national states were weak or non-existent, they had to be 'built'.

At least until the late 1960s, there was a good deal of optimism about both the economic capacity and democratic potential of the new state machines burgeoning in ex-colonial territories. The counter-trends of the 1960s – pervasive corruption, the ineffectiveness or distorted impact of national 'planning', widespread authoritarianism or political instability, and dis-

* Institute of Development Studies at the University of Sussex.

appointing socio-economic performance – undermined simpler statist conceptions of the development process. During the 1970s, a number of key debates emerged, initiated by spokesmen from both ends of the ideological spectrum. Neo-classical analysts have questioned the advisability of widespread state economic intervention and drawn our attention to the costs of state-directed strategies of industrialisation, notably the model of import-substituting industrialisation (for example, see Deepak Lal's critique of 'dirigiste dogma' [*1983*]). Neo-Marxist and many dependency analysts have focused on the class character and international linkages of Third World states, arguing for radical social transformation and new socialist state institutions as the preconditions for 'real' development, productively more rational and distributively more fair (Bienefeld and Godfrey [*1982*] review the debates). The debates have helped to focus attention more precisely on the problematic of the developmental state – its social basis, institutional forms, modes of operation and developmental impact.

They have brought greater clarity to thinking about the economic role of the state, and greater sobriety about the practical possibilities of state involvement in the industrialisation process. Any general notion that rapid industrialisation could be achieved simply through more 'planning' and more extensive state involvement has been thoroughly undermined by both theory and historical experience. The developmental strength of any particular state cannot be equated with its size, coercive apparatus, ideological aura or institutional character. If one controls for environmental differences, the 'strength' of a developmental state, specifically (in the context of this article) its ability to intervene positively to foster industrialisation, rests on three basic factors:

(i) Its *social nature*: the social character and political interests of the groups which direct and compose the state and the nature of their links with domestic and international forces (for a useful review of these issues in the Tanzanian case, see Saul [*1979*]). To the extent that the state rests on, or embodies, social forces favourable to industrialisation, it gains in credibility and effect. Clarity on this question helps to explain particular patterns of state action and dispel some of the confusion arising from the frequent mismatch between proclaimed goals and actual impact. If we know on whose behalf a given state is acting, we have a more substantive idea of its 'effectiveness'.

There is immense variation in the social interests served by state action. Broadly, state action may embody the interests of three different forces: (a) The *state itself* as a matrix of distinct 'autonomous' interests, more or less homogeneous. This reality is captured by the idea of 'die Staatsklasse' in central European political theory; in a Third World context, by various more or less cogent notions of a state-based 'petty-bourgeoisie' or 'office-holders of capital' within 'dependent capitalist' regimes [*Cardoso, 1979: 210*] or 'bureaucratic bourgeoisie' in intermediate regimes [*Shivji, 1975; Meillassoux, 1970*] and of a 'red bourgeoisie' or 'privileged stratum' in state socialist contexts (for example, in Maoist analyses of the Chinese state [*G. White, 1983a*]). In certain contexts, state interest (or specific interests within a heterogeneous state) may define rapid industrialisation as their own over-riding aim; in turn, industrialisation may consolidate and extend the material basis of state power. Such a symbiosis may be positive to the extent that it overcomes obstacles to industrialisation posed by conservative classes, absence of an entrepreneurial stratum, lack of social cohesion or national sovereignty. It may be negative to the extent that it disregards other claimants to the fruits of development and becomes linked to a rigid and/or inappropriate pattern of industrialisation (for example, overemphasis on heavy industry, neglect or exploitation of agriculture, or over-accumulation); (b) A *hegemonic class or class coalition*: here we do not mean that the state 'represents' class interests, in a reductionist sense, but, in Cardoso's words [*1979: 209*] it 'unites dominant classes in the exercise of domination over the rest of society'. It both reflects and transcends the interests of the dominant classes. Clearly, basic strategies of industrialisation (notably investment priorities, types of industrial institutions adopted, trade regimes, etc.) and the pattern of injured/advanced social interests depend heavily on the nature of this class configuration. In societies where dominant classes are divided or deadlocked, or where the political crystallisation of class forces is weak, there is scope for the emergence of state autonomy and the assertion of state interest (for example, Marxist analysis of the Bonapartist State, discussed by Alavi [*1972*]). (c) The *nation vis-à-vis* other nations, that is, the state as asserting an independent 'national interest' which is not mere ideological camouflage, as cruder Marxist analysts would argue, but a reflection of the historical and cultural reality of a discrete 'material' entity, the nation [*Debray, 1977*]. As such, the state embodies a power bloc independent from, and often opposed to, interests external to the society. In this context, industrialisation – capitalist, socialist or 'intermediate' – is the means whereby a formerly exploited and/or backward nation 'catches up' with the industrialised nations, capitalist or socialist [*Ellman, 1979: 272-73*]. The state is an instrument of international redistribution.

(ii) The state's *politico-adminstrative capacity*: we can distinguish three dimensions: (a) Its *political* capacity to define and disseminate a new ideology of 'industrialism' (what Gerschenkron [*1966: 25*] calls a 'New Deal in emotions'), provide stable and dynamic leadership and mobilise widespread support for industrialisation programmes. Both neo-Marxist and more conventional analysts (e.g., *Huntington, 1968*) have emphasised the crucial need for a developmental state to achieve a certain 'autonomy' from social forces (for the notion of 'autonomy', see Skocpol [*1979*]). Although a specific industrialisation programme may reflect the interests of a particular class or class coalition, effective state action often depends on its ability to transcend those interests at any given time (e.g., a socialist government keeping industrial wages low in a 'workers' state', or a state capitalist regime putting heavy pressure on sectors of the bourgeoisie, as in South Korea's industrial restructuring in the 1970s); (b) The existence of reasonably efficient *administrative* institutions responsive to political cues, resistant to penetration by special interests and relatively free from the perennial problems of complex bureaucratic organisations; (c) a *technical* capacity to analyse problems, formulate feasible solutions and implement them in technically competent ways. This would include planning expertise, reliable statistical procedures, etc. These three aspects of politico-administrative capacity are interrelated and mutually reinforcing in practice; these are the factors which analysts such as Myrdal [*1970*] use to distinguish 'hard' and 'soft' states and which condition the state's capacity for consistent and comprehensive planning [cf. *World Bank, 1983*].

(iii) The *specific modes of involvement* of state organisations in social and economic processes to further industrialisation: (for useful reviews, see Sutcliffe [*1971: Chap. 8*] and Szostak [*1983*]). We can broadly distinguish two types of involvement: parametric and pervasive. *Parametric* measures imply a certain amount of autonomy on the part of economic actors and processes; the state's role is limited to providing a framework of institutions and resources conducive to industrialisation. One can distinguish three forms of parametric action: first, the familiar *regulative* processes of macro-economic management (interest rates, tariffs, subsidies, taxation, etc.), taking more or less direct forms, and charged with providing both a stable matrix for the operation of markets and correctives for market failures; second, the establishment of an *institutional* context favourable to industrialisation (for example, a responsive financial system, or a systematic legal framework); third, in the *infrastructural* sense, the state lays down the material (communications, energy, basic construction) and human (education, technique, health) preconditions for industrialisation.

Through *pervasive* measures, state organisations become more directly involved in processes of industrial investment, production and circulation, eliminating or circumscribing the autonomy of economic actors. This takes two familiar forms: (i) administrative, that is, the extension into industry of bureaucratic organisations, regionally or functionally based, underpinned juridically by state ownership of industrial means of production or financial institutions and responsible for supervising public corporations endowed with varying degrees of autonomy; (ii) *political*, that is, the direct or indirect economic impact of political organisations (be they political parties, armies, or mass organisations). At the micro-level, this may involve the establishment of political control networks in industrial enterprises and bureaux; at the macro-level, political action plays a *class* role by constructing the basic social preconditions for industrialisation (by mobilising and controlling labour, strengthening the social power of accumulating strata, destroying or undermining classes inimical to industrialisation). Thus, in a capitalist context, the state may strive to establish a 'social structure of accumulation' by nurturing the emergence of financial and industrial bourgeoisie and collaborating with capital in establishing the subordination of labour so crucial for sustained capitalist accumulation (for the Mexican example, see Bennett and Sharpe [*1980*]).

Pervasive intervention involves different types and degrees of state penetration of industrial processes: direct managerial controls over investment, production and exchange, as in the Soviet system of industrial administration whereby productive units are allowed little economic initiative; mediated controls through various types of parastatals or quasi-autonomous bodies which are state-owned but enjoy varying degrees of operational independence; organisation of and control over intermediate economic associations which may be formally independent (for example, certain forms of 'corporatism', see Schmitter and Lehmbruch [*1980*]; Cardoso's concept of 'bureaucratic rings' in Latin America [*1979: 215*]; the development and manipulation of industrial associations or cartels in South Korea and Taiwan). From the reams that have been written about the relative merits of these two forms of state involvement in the economy, three interesting points emerge. First, there are developmental dangers on the side of the minimally parametric (market failures) and the maximally pervasive state (bureaucratic failures) – some balance needs to be struck. Second, the nature of this developmentally advisable balance varies across societies and within the same society over time – in general, pervasive methods have been more characteristic of earlier phases of the industrialisation process. Third, that the basic problem of modes and degree of state involvement is common to widely varying social systems, although the issues may be discussed in different vocabularies (government intervention versus free enterprise in capitalist contexts, state versus market or civil society in socialist contexts).

Hopefully, the above distinctions help to unravel some of the complexity of state involvement in industrialisation. At the simplest level, they can be used to construct a typology of developmental states. Though the classical liberal state – whether in its weak 'umpire' or strong 'catalytic' versions – exists as a category, as a historical phenomenon it is rare indeed. Most currently lauded models of 'free enterprise' or 'market-orientated' development turn out to have embarrassingly pervasive states. In one favourite case, the Ivory Coast, the state owned 53 per cent of the total 'social capital of enterprises' in 1982 [*Ikonnicoff, 1983: 17*]; arch-NIC Taiwan is the only country I know of with a capitalist economy and a Leninist state which, in Amsden's words, 'has acted as a key agent in the process of capital accumulation' [*1979: 342*]; 'liberal' Hong Kong is, after all, a colony.

It is relatively easy to expose the empirical shortcomings of authors who champion such countries as living embodiments of the neo-classical case, by demonstrating that markets have been systematically structured or circumscribed by state action. However, any evaluation of the liberal story (notably on the 'East Asian NIC model'), must probe into deeper analytical failings, namely the apparent naivety or myopia of neo-classical authors when addressing the question of states and markets. First, they fail adequately to problematise the concepts of both markets and states. Markets tend to be analysed as 'economic' processes, rather than as dynamic social systems which are matrices of competing interests and clusters of power. States, to the extent that they are analysed independently at all, tend to be seen as relatively neutral, 'national' entities, treated anthropomorphically ('South Korea decided ...', etc.) and described as playing a mainly 'catalytic' developmental role from 'outside' the economy. Good or bad 'public policies' are seen as emerging from rational or irrational decision-making (often

plus some vague cultural trait), without penetrating to the arenas of conflict-
ing social forces and politico-bureaucratic interests which determine the
policy agenda in the first place. For example, Little [*1979: 4*] exemplifies this
kind of superficiality when he argues that the success of the East Asian NICs
'is almost entirely due to good policies and the ability of the people'. To the
extent that politics is included in the analysis of state policy, it is treated as an
exogenous desideratum (the old chestnut 'political will') or described in
terms of a rarefied, and rather wishful, model of the 'social contract' (for
example, see Ranis [*1974; 1982*] on the Philippines and on Taiwan/South
Korea). Where the authoritarianism of NIC regimes is recognised, it is
deodorised as 'strong, stable government' [*Little, 1979: 6*].

Second, liberal economic analysts operate within a conventional ideological framework of analysis which separates states from markets, politics
from economics and which views the state as an entity alien to the economy,
except in strictly specified circumstances. Hence the use of the term
'intervention' with its unfavourable loading. When analysing actual and
desirable patterns of political economy, the separation of state and economy
is an important focus of inquiry, but it cannot be *assumed* either descriptively
or prescriptively, especially when analysing societies (such as South Korea
or Taiwan) where ideological assumptions about the 'natural' relationship
between state and economy may be very different, if not opposite. Even in
Western capitalist contexts, moreover, the intellectual polarisation of an
'interventionist state' *vis-à-vis* 'free markets' should be questioned. As
Cairncross has argued in the British context, the increasing role of the state
'does not in the main reflect ideological antipathy to reliance on market
forces', rather the pressure for the expanded controls necessary to maintain
a social context within which 'free enterprise' capitalism, and therefore
'market forces' can continue to operate [*Cairncross, 1976: 132, cited in Smith
and Wood, 1982: 8*].

Third, liberal analysts fail to investigate the real-world relationships
between 'free' markets and dictatorial politics. In key areas of economic life,
most notably labour markets (but also, for example, the 'liberalisation' of
trade regimes), economic liberalism appears to depend on political authoritarianism. 'Free' labour markets in countries like South Korea or Taiwan
have been enforced by political unfreedom – consistently repressive and
intermittently vicious controls over labour unions or manifestations of
labour 'unrest'. Little sidesteps the issue neatly by inverting it, referring to
the 'absence of union pressure ... or government intervention in favour of
high wages' [*1979: 28*]. If we invert *our* argument, we could make a strong
case that greater political democracy in fact makes for greater economic
'interventionism' by the state because it is prompted to action by the pressures of diverse and autonomous interest groups.

In the real world of developmental states, it is possible to distinguish three
broad types, each of which has a distinctive class character and pattern of
intervention: (i) 'state capitalist' countries, in which the relationship
between state and private capital involves both control and collaboration
and where the state itself acts as an economic entrepreneur and exercises a
wide range of direct and indirect controls over economic actors; (ii)

'intermediate regimes', identified by Kalecki [*1967: cf. Petras, 1977*] which, often using 'socialist' labels, severely circumscribe the power of private industrial capital and base industrialisation on a massive expansion of state ownership and management, the 'state-class' emerging as a crucially independent interest to dominate those of civil society; (iii) state socialist regimes where private industrial capital is largely eliminated, controls are all-pervasive and the state, in its initial stages at least, represents the interests and aspirations of the revolutionary coalition (which varies from country to country; compare the social composition of winning coalitions in the Soviet Union, China and Cuba). In reality, the dividing line between these three categories is blurred; each category contains a great deal of internal variation and requires further specification. Within the state-capitalist category, for example, there are important differences in the form of the state and state-class relations between, say, the Philippines, Brazil or Kenya. Even in cases of superficial similarity, such as South Korea and Taiwan, closer scrutiny reveals significant differences. Here I shall focus on the role of the state in industrialisation in the third category, state socialist societies.

This diversity undermines the validity of general judgements about *the* role of *the* state in industrialisation and general policy prescriptions which flow from them – whether they call for 'more' or 'less' state involvement. Clearly questions of 'more' or 'less' must be situated in a concrete analysis of specific states which discusses not merely forms and degrees of intervention, but also their social character and politico-administrative capacity. Analyses which tend to concentrate on one or the other of these factors are of limited utility, whether they be neo-Marxist political economy which focuses primarily on the social nature of the state, conventional political science on the state itself, or conventional development economics on specific forms of intervention. Policy analysis should be rooted in all three dimensions of the state and policy prescriptions tailored to its specific capacities and inclinations in particular national circumstances. In short, one should look not merely at the proximate determinants of policy, but also the deeper over-determinants, at 'non-decisions' as well as decisions.

Before turning to state socialism in particular, let us cast a brief look at the overall historical context of Third World industrialisation over the past three decades. The experience of this phase, combined with that of the first wave of 'late development' in the late nineteenth and early twentieth centuries, support one firm conclusion: that whilst a high degree of state intervention, both paramatric *and* pervasive, not only economic but social and political, is not a sufficient condition for successful industrialisation, it is at least a necessary condition. This conclusion demonstrates the need to see industrialisation as a profound social and political and not merely economic phenomenon. The stars in the firmament of late industrialisation, socialist or capitalist – the Soviet Union, Japan, South and North Korea, Taiwan, Brazil – provide strong empirical support for this conclusion. The experience of successful state capitalist industrialisers points to the crucial importance of an 'autonomous' state which exercises some form of strategic coordination and control over central elements and agents of industrialisation

[*Evans and Alizadeh, 1984*]. State action may be economic (some form of overall planning, mobilisation of savings, allocation of priority investments, public ownership in key sectors, regulation of international flows of commodities, finance and technology); political (negatively through controls over labour organisation and suppression of competing developmental programmes, or positively through mobilisation of popular support or at least acquiescence through ideological appeals) and social, establishing the 'social structure of accumulation' by altering the balance of power between classes and transforming social attitudes.

Such plaudits for the role of states are highly conditional – the relationship between state action and industrialisation is very complex and unambiguous success stories are still rare. Moreover, even where a state's role may be positive in early industrialisation, it may become less so in later stages. Let us examine some of these issues in more detail in the context of state socialist societies.

II: THE STATE AND SOCIALIST INDUSTRIALISATION IN THE THIRD WORLD

There are many forms of 'socialist' regime in the Third World (for a general discussion, see G. White [*1983b: 1-9*]). I make a basic distinction between 'state socialist' nations – revolutionary systems in the Marxist–Leninist tradition, and various types of 'intermediate regime'. I shall concentrate on the former but some of my analysis may have some relevance to the latter, even though their institutional and social characters differ. Table 1 provides an overview of the basic national characteristics and industrial performance of both state socialist and socialist intermediate regimes in Eastern Europe and the Third World.

State socialist systems themselves differ widely in size, economic structure and industrial performance. There is an important distinction between relatively long-lived and well-established cases (such as North Korea, Mongolia, China and Vietnam) and more recent cases (such as Angola, South Yemen, Mozambique and Nicaragua). Since I am seeking to understand the underlying dynamics of state-sponsored socialist industrialisation, I shall concentrate on the former group drawing also on Eastern European experience where relevant. My conclusions affect the latter group, however, and I shall return to them in a later section.

Marxist socialist definitions of development have emphasised the crucial historical significance of rapid and comprehensive industrialisation. At the most abstract level, industrialisation has been defined as an essential precondition for the achievement of 'full' socialism in at least four senses: *economically* as creating the material conditions for an ultimate transition from scarcity to abundance, from economic to social calculation, from the realm of necessity to the realm of freedom; *politically* as the means to establish the social base of mature socialism, the industrial working class; *culturally* as underpinning the social advancement of the population which is a necessary condition for personal emancipation and collective endeavour. Since revolutionary socialism has been successful in contexts of relative underdevelopment – as a response to internal backwardness and international subordination – industrialisation has also been viewed in *national* terms as an essential defence against the politico-military hostility of imperialist powers and a means to catch up economically with industrialised capitalist nations.

Given this distinct historical form of socialism (Chinese theorists call it 'backward' or 'underdeveloped socialism') the post-revolutionary state has become the main *animateur* and organiser of industrialisation. On the one hand, this reflects the general phenomenon of 'late development'; on the other, it reflects the distinctive aims and social dynamics of socialist development, that is, the state as the source of new ideology of 'industrialism' (Lane [*1974*] identifies Leninism as 'the development ethic of Marxism'), as an alternative to the bourgeoisie as an agent of accumulation, as organisational expression of the interests of the revolutionary coalition, as institutional embodiment of the logic of comprehensive planning, and as a security apparatus against inimical international pressure (cf. Nove's idea of 'developmental socialism'; [*1983: 183-96*]). The case for a pervasive state in the first crucial stages of socialist industrialisation has been a strong one. Even so, the specific nature of state institutions and policies in the crucial 'genetic' period of state construction is still a focus of debate and choice. Any rationale for a pervasive state, moreover, is historically transient; the theory (if not the practice) of revolutionary socialism requires that the state be transitional, preparing the conditions for its own supersession.

(i) The Soviet Model

Turning to the historical experience of socialist industrialisation, it is important to clarify the impact of the Soviet example, the first embodiment of socialist industrialisation and model for later programmes, whether emulated or enforced. As a system of social control, political mobilisation, capital accumulation and economic management, the Soviet model was heavily statist in conception and practice, with a politically and economically pervasive authoritarian state, mobilising and allocating surplus through imperative plans and managing industry directly through administrative bureaux and public enterprises. As a development strategy, it was relatively autarkic/autarchic in both execution and aims, premised on the enforced necessity of predominantly internal sources of accumulation; it gave heavy industry priority over light, and industry over agriculture.

While we may affirm these main dimensions of the model, we must be careful to avoid a stereotype. The strategy was not wholly 'self-reliant'; external credits were received during the First Five-Year Plan and agricultural exports were used to finance imports of capital goods. Moreover, the familiar theme of industry exploiting agriculture and cities draining the countryside during the First Five-Year Plan has been questioned on strong empirical grounds [*Ellman, 1975*]. Although modern technique was lionised, the technological strategy actually adopted was dualistic. Finally, new industry was not constructed *ex nihilo* but on the basis of considerable existing industrial and technical capacity.

It is also important not to see this initial model as the product of develop-

TABLE 1

INDUSTRIALISATION IN STATE SOCIALIST AND SOCIALIST INTERMEDIATE CONTEXTS

Type Of Country	Population (Millions) Mid-1980	GNP Per Capita 1980 (Dollars)	Average Annual Growth In GNP Per Capita 1960-80	Industrial Output As Percentage Of GDP 1960	Industrial Output As Percentage Of GDP 1980	Manufacturing Output As Percentage Of GDP 1960	Manufacturing Output As Percentage Of GDP 1980	Average Annual Growth Rate Of Industry (%) '60-70	Average Annual Growth Rate Of Industry (%) '70-80	Average Annual Growth Rate Of Manufactures (%) '60-70	Average Annual Growth Rate Of Manufactures (%) '70-80	Labour Force In Industry (%) 1960	Labour Force In Industry (%) 1980
Industrialised Marxist-Leninist Socialist Countries:													
Bulgaria	9.0	4,150	5.6	53	58	46	-		7.6			25	39
Czechoslovakia	15.3	5,820	4.0	73	75	63	-		5.7			46	48
German DR	16.9	7,180	4.7	-	70	-	-		5.8			48	50
Hungary	10.8	4,180	4.5	69	59	59	-		4.9			35	53
Poland	35.8	3,900	5.3	57	64	47	-		7.5			29	39
Soviet Union	265.5	4,550	4.0	62	62	52	-					29	45
Industrialising Marxist-Leninist Socialist Countries													
(a) Middle-income													
Albania	2.7	-	-	-	-							18	25
Angola	7.1	470	-2.3	8	23	4	3	11.0	-3.9	7.2	-12.0	12	16
Congo	1.6	900	0.8	17	45	10	6	7.0	4.0	6.8	-	17	26
Cuba	9.7	810	-	65	67				7.9			22	31
Korea DPR	18.3	-	6.7						15.9			23	33
Mongolia	1.7	-	-									13	22
Romania	22.2	2,340	8.6	-	64	-	-	12.8	9.7			15	36
Yemen PDR	1.9	420	12.1	-	28	-	14				7.0	15	15
(b) Low-income													
Afghanistan	15.9	-	-	8	12	3	7					6	8
Benin	3.4	310	0.4	-	-	-	-					9	16
China	976.7	290	-	12	47	-	11	11.2	8.7			-	17
Ethiopia	31.1	140	1.4	-	16	6	-	7.4	1.4	8.0	2.4	5	7
Kampuchia	6.9	-	-	-	-	-	-					4	-
Laos	3.4	-	-	-	-	-	-					4	6
Mozambique	12.1	230	-0.1	9	16	8	9	9.5	-5.6	6.5	-5.8	8	18
Vietnam	54.2	160	-	-	-	-	-					-	10

TABLE 1 (continued)

INDUSTRIALISATION IN STATE SOCIALIST AND SOCIALIST INTERMEDIATE CONTEXTS

Type Of Country	Population (Millions) Mid-1980	GNP Per Capita 1980 (Dollars)	Average Annual Growth In GNP Per Capita 1960-80	Industrial Output As Percentage Of GDP		Manufacturing Output As Percentage Of GDP		Average Annual Growth Rate Of Industry (%)		Average Annual Growth Rate Of Manufactures (%)		Labour Force In Industry (%)	
				1960	1980	1960	1980	'60-70	'70-80	'60-70	'70-80	1960	1980
Industrialising Socialist "intermediate regimes"													
(a) Middle-income													
Algeria	18.9	1,870	3.2	35	57	6	14	11.6	7.9	7.8	11.4	12	25
Iraq	13.1	3,020	5.3	52	73	10	6	4.7	-	5.9	-	18	26
Libya	3.0	8,640	5.2	-	72	-	4	-	-2.3	-	18.9	17	28
Nicaragua	2.6	740	0.9	21	31	16	25	10.4	2.2	11.4	2.9	16	14
Syria (?)	9.0	1,340	3.7	-	27	-	21	-	9.6	-	7.9	19	31
Tunisia (?)	6.4	1,310	4.8	18	35	8	13	8.2	9.0	7.8	11.2	18	33
Yugoslavia	22.3	2,620	5.4	45	43	36	30	6.2	7.1	5.7	7.3	18	35
Zambia	5.8	560	0.2	63	39	4	17	-	0.1	-	0.4	7	11
Zimbabwe	7.4	630	0.7	35	39	17	25	-	1.8	-	2.8	11	15
(b) Low-income													
Burma	34.8	170	1.2	12	13	8	10	3.1	5.2	3.7	4.4	10	10
Guinea	5.4	290	0.3	-	33	-	4	-	-	-	-	6	11
Madagascar	8.7	350	-0.5	10	18	4	-	-	1.0	-	-	2	3
Somalia	3.9	-	-	8	11	3	7	3.4	-2.6	4.0	-3.8	4	8
Sudan (?)	18.7	410	-0.2	-	14	-	6	-	3.1	-	1.3	6	10
Tanzania	18.7	280	1.9	11	13	5	9	-	1.9	-	3.6	4	6

Sources: IBRD, *World Development Report 1982*; Gordon White, Robin Murray and Christine White (eds.), *Revolutionary Socialist Development in the Third World*, Harvester Press, 1983; Jan Vanous, 'East European Economic Slowdown', *Problems of Communism*, XXXI:4 (July–Aug. 1982), pp.1-19.

mental choice, pure and simple. In the momentous debates of the 1920s, the logic of argument was increasingly stifled by the logic of circumstance, the mounting pressures of internal social conflict and external politico-military pressure. Moreover, while the model was faulty in conception and execution and calamitous in its human effects, its undeniable success as a mechanism of rapid industrialisation heavily depended on specific characteristics of the Soviet Union – its large size, diversified resource base, stock of materials and human capital, and state tradition.

The character of the strategy, and of the state which accompanied it, were complementary and mutually reinforcing. The external threat, the assault on the peasantry, the need to generate high levels of savings, to concentrate industrial resources and discipline the new industrial workforce – all these factors conspired to strengthen the argument for, and the reality of, a pervasive state. Once established, a familiar process was set in train. A sea-change took place as the authoritarian post-revolutionary state (seen as necessary but transitional, and drawing its power from the awesome nature of the tasks it was tackling) gradually came to act not merely to solve developmental problems but also to protect or further its own power – the transformation of *raison d'être* into *raison d'état*. In class terms, this was a transition from something resembling a workers' state which emerged from the October Revolution to an increasingly (but not fully) apparatchik state in the 1930s.

(ii) The First Wave of Third World Socialist Industrialisation

As an engine of industrial growth, the Soviet model has been successful in the Soviet Union and Eastern Europe in creating a second tier of industrialised nations which produce an increasing share of global manufacturing output; it was less than 10 per cent at the end of the Second World War, and rose from 18 per cent in 1960 to more than 27 per cent in 1975 [*UNIDO, 1979*]. It is hardly surprising, therefore, that this statist conception of socialist industrialisation was very attractive to the first wave of socialist Third World countries (notably China, Korea and Vietnam). It was seen not only as a way out of backwardness but also as an appropriate response to international conditions in the late 1940s and 1950s. Global confrontation and military pressure made 'self-reliance' seem economically sensible and rapid industrialisation politically essential. These early socialist governments did not face a neo-classical world of more or less convenient complementarities; the applicability of conventional theories of specialisation and comparative cost was very limited. State-sponsored crash industrialisation was a basic condition not merely for economic progress (particularly if a country did not want to become dependent on the Soviet Union), but also for national survival.

The classic Soviet model has been applied reasonably successfully in certain Third World countries. Size and resource endowment have been crucial factors, the strategy obviously working better in a large, comprehensively endowed economy, the best example being China. For smaller economies, application was more problematic, but the North Korean case was remarkably successful, at least until the mid-1970s (*G. White, 1982; Halliday, 1983*]. Tables 2 and 3 give a summary idea of their performance.

Each has maintained generally high rates of industrial growth and established a relatively comprehensive industrial structure within a framework of import substitution. In each case, one could argue that the classic pattern of socialist industrialisation brought them into the ranks of the 'newly industrialised countries' (NICs). The degree of structural change was more thoroughgoing in the Korean case: industry was over 60 per cent of GNP by the early 1970s and industrial employment reached 33 per cent of the total workforce by 1980, compared to 47 per cent and 19 per cent respectively in China (both 1981) [*World Bank, 1983; Far Eastern Economic Review, 1983*]. Ironically, despite earlier claims about the distinctiveness of the 'Chinese model', Chinese performance reflects classical Soviet priorities with heavy industry growing twice as fast as light. North Korea, on the other hand, seems to have maintained a better balance between heavy industry, light industry and agriculture (for example, see Chung [*1974: Tables 23-4*]).

However, the Soviet model had certain features which clashed sharply with the characteristic endowments and capacities of most Third World countries. At the strategic level, it privileged advanced technology and large-scale production which posed problems in labour-surplus countries with low levels of human capital formation and limited import capacity; it tended to see agriculture, especially small-scale agriculture, as an obstacle rather than an impetus to industrialisation, a rickety foundation for any development strategy in predominantly agricultural societies; its stress on industry over commerce and heavy over light industry could exacerbate employment problems and starve agriculture of the goods necessary to stimulate work incentives; a stress on 'self-reliance' which made sense in a continental economy, ill-accorded with the realities of small, imbalanced, trade-dependent economies.

Focusing specifically on the *role of the state*, there have been four problems: first, over-reliance on political mobilisation and directive planning brings increasingly heavy costs resulting from mis-allocation, waste, inflexibility and 'voluntaristic' policy errors. Second, in countries with scarce educated manpower and poor communications, it is very difficult to establish comprehensive and efficient planning systems in the short- and even medium-term. Even in a country such as China, with a strong bureaucratic tradition and capacity, it is still (as of 1983) hard to argue that there is an effective 'central planning system'. Third, the political authoritarianism of the model becomes self-perpetuating and resistant to democratisation. Fourth, prolonged stress on 'self-reliance' may well convert economic autarky from a means into an end of development policy, fostering a chauvinist state which justifies its dominance in terms of external threat and rejects opportunities for increasing international ties.

These problems intensified during the 1960s and 1970s as changes took place within each country and in the world at large. First, the very *success* of the classic pattern of industrialisation meant that, as the economy grew more complex and sources of extensive growth began to dwindle [*Wilczynski, 1972: Chap. 2*], the characteristic problems of pervasive state intervention

TABLE 2

MAIN INDICES OF CHINESE ECONOMIC PERFORMANCE

	1	2	3	4	5	6	7	8	9
Year	Annual Growth in GNP (%)	GNP per cap (1978 dollars)[1]	Gross domestic investment as % of GDP	Index of agri-cultural pro-duction (1952 = 100)	Annual growth in agri-cultural pro-duction (%)	Index of indust-rial pro-duction (1952 = 100)	Annual growth of indust-rial pro-duction (1952 = 100)	Index of heavy industry pro-duction (1952 = 100)	Index of light industry pro-duction (1952 = 100)
1949	–	108.9		67.3		40.8		30.3	46.6
1950	22.0	130.4		79.2	17.8	55.7	36.4	46.7	60.6
1951	16.7	149.2		86.6	9.4	77.0	38.2	69.7	81.0
1952	17.9	172.2	19.6	100.0	15.2	100.0	29.9	100.0	100.0
1953	6.1	178.6 ⎫		103.1	3.1	130.3	30.3	136.9	126.7
1954	4.8	182.8 ⎬ 21.9 (ave)		106.6	3.4	151.6	16.3	163.9	144.8
1955	9.1	195.2 ⎬		114.8	7.6	160.1	5.6	187.7	144.8
1956	8.3	207.0 ⎭		120.4	5.0	204.9	28.1	262.3	173.3
1957	6.2	213.4	23.0	124.8	3.6	228.6	11.5	310.7	183.2
1958	18.8	249.0	30.7	127.8	2.4	353.8	54.8	555.5	245.0
1959	–4.9	232.5	39.3	110.4	–13.6	481.8	36.1	822.7	299.0
1960	–2.6	222.4	35.5	96.4	–12.6	535.7	11.2	1040.0	269.5
1961	–21.1	173.5	24.4	94.0	–2.4	330.7	–38.2	553.6	211.1
1962	9.2	187.1	10.9	100.0	6.2	275.9	–16.6	428.4	193.5
1963	13.0	208.9 ⎫		111.6	11.6	299.4	8.5	487.8	198.1
1964	10.8	228.8 ⎬ 19.6 (ave)		126.7	13.5	358.3	19.6	590.3	233.4
1965	12.8	255.0 ⎭	25.1	137.1	8.3	452.6	26.4	650.6	344.5
1966	13.5	282.1 ⎫		148.9	8.6	547.4	20.9	829.5	394.3
1967	–3.8	264.5 ⎬ 23.3 (ave)		151.3	1.6	471.8	–13.8	663.6	366.4
1968	1.0	260.3 ⎬		147.5	–2.5	448.0	–5.0	629.8	348.3
1969	10.8	281.0 ⎭		149.2	1.1	601.6	34.3	906.6	436.1
1970	16.4	318.7	30.4	166.4	11.5	786.0	30.7	1290.0	514.9
1971	6.8	333.2	31.6	171.4	3.1	903.3	14.9	1570.0	548.2
1972	4.6	341.2	29.6	171.1	–0.2	962.9	6.6	1680.0	582.2
1973	12.9	377.0 ⎫		185.5	8.4	1050.0	9.5	1820.0	643.6
1974	3.6	382.2 ⎭ 30.7 (ave)		193.2	4.2	1060.0	0.3	1790.0	660.6
1975	7.0	400.1	31.6	202.1	4.6	1220.0	15.1	2090.0	746.4
1976	0.0	394.6	29.5	207.1	2.5	1230.0	1.3	2100.0	766.4
1977	8.2	421.1	30.5	210.6	1.7	1410.0	14.3	2400.0	873.7
1978	11.6	463.4	33.8	229.6	9.0	1600.0	13.5	2780.0	968.1
1979	5.4	482.0	31.3	249.4	8.6	1730.0	8.5	2990.0	1060.0
1980	6.8	508.9	30.6	256.1	2.7	1880.0	8.7	3030.0	1250.0
1981	3.0	516.9	28.7	270.7	5.7	1960.0	4.1	2890.0	1430.0
Overall Average	7.3		26.6		4.7		14.4		
	(1)	(2)	(3)	(4)	(5)	(6)	(7)	(8)	(9)

Note: 1) US Government estimates

Source: Compiled from tables in Willy Kraus, *Economic Development and Social Change in the PRC*, New York: Springer-Verlag, 1982, pp. 325ff.

multiplied. Second, to the extent that a more complex economy generates pressures for increasing foreign trade (especially in smaller countries like North Korea or Hungary), international competitive pressures generated demands for more flexible economic management and more dynamic technological progress. These trends have reflected domestic *political* pressures, notably discontent arising from 'postponed' consumption. New generations were unimpressed by the erstwhile (and often ersatz) virtues of revolutionary austerity and found the arguments for economic and political authoritarianism less and less convincing. The international political environment also became less threatening during the 1960s and early 1970s and opportunities

TABLE 3

MAIN INDICES OF NORTH KOREAN ECONOMIC PERFORMANCE

Year	Growth of GNP (%)	Growth of Grain[a] Production (%)	Growth of Industrial[b] Production (%)
1947–49	-	12	50
1950–53	-	−3	−11
1954–56	-	7	42
1957–60	-	7	36
1961–65	10	3	14
1966–70	6	2	11
1971–73	11	2	17
1974	12	31	18
1975	8	10	20
1976	−3	4	10
1977	negl.	6	11
1978	7	negl.	17
1947–65	7	5	22
1966–78	6	5	14

Notes: (a) based on official grain figures
       (b) official figures (gross value in current prices)

Sources: CIA, Handbook of Economic Statistics, 1979, Washington DC; J. Chung, *The North Korean Economy, Structure and Development*, Stanford, Cal., 1974.

for 'normal' intercourse with capitalist countries increased (Vietnam is a notable exception here).

In successful socialist industrialisers, such as China or North Korea (like their Eastern European counterparts), these internal and external politico-economic pressures have combined to create a new set of strategic policy challenges. As the trajectory of their development path moves from extensive toward intensive, and from import substitution toward export-orientation, issues of micro-economic efficiency and technological dynamism take on cardinal significance. The implications for the economic role of the socialist state are profound, as we shall see in section III.

(iii) The Second Wave of Third World Socialist Industrialisers

In most cases, revolutionary socialist regimes established in the 1960s and 1970s (notably Angola, Mozambique, Ethiopia, South Yemen and Nicaragua) were in relatively small, trade-dependent, agriculture-dominated territories which are unsuitable contexts for the classic model of socialist industrialisation. Theoretical and policy debates in these countries centre on the need to devise new strategies of 'socialist development' consonant with their specific economic endowments, socio-political capacity, and international environment. Although their revolutionary elites retain the ultimate aim of industrialisation, they must chart different paths which involve heavy stress on agriculture and agro-industry and on the international (predominantly capitalist) economy.

Cuba is an early example of an export-orientated and agriculture-based path to industrialisation and its ambiguous record illustrates the difficulties

TABLE 4

GROSS MATERIALS PRODUCT BY SECTORS OF ECONOMIC ACTIVITY[a]

	1970	1971	1972	1973	1974	1975	1976	1977	1978
					Millions of constant pesos				
Total material product	5666	5904	6478	7328	7900	8868	9210	9555	10,353
Rural sector	1230	1153	1216	1271	1328	1394	1468	1565	1675
Industry	4000	4177	4458	4988	5393	6067	6250	6337	6914
Construction	436	574	804	1069	1179	1407	1492	1653	1767
					Composition (%)				
Total material product	100.0	100.0	100.0	100.0	100.0	100.0	100.0	100.0	100.0
Rural sector	21.7	19.5	18.8	17.3	16.8	15.7	15.9	16.4	16.2
Industry	70.6	70.8	68.8	68.1	68.3	68.4	67.9	66.3	66.8
Construction	7.7	9.7	12.4	14.6	14.9	15.9	16..2	17.3	17.0
					Growth rates				
Total material product		4.2	9.7	13.1	7.8	12.3	3.9	3.7	8.4
Rural sector		6.3	5.5	4.5	4.5	5.0	5.3	6.3	7.0
Industry		4.4	6.7	11.9	8.1	12.5	3.0	1.4	9.1
Construction		31.7	40.1	33.0	10.3	19.3	6.0	10.8	6.9

Note: (a) Gross Material Product equals the gross output of the 'productive' sectors: rural
sector, fishing, mining, manufacture, construction and electricity.

Source: CEPAL, Cuba: Motal para el Estudio Economico de America Latina: 1978, 1980
[cited in Carciofi, 1983: 205].

of socialist development for small nations in 'peripheral' conditions. Basic
data for the 1970s are presented in Table 4.

Carciofi's [1983] analysis of these data points to substantial success but
continuing constraints and problems which have brought increasing concern
in the early 1980s. Progress in mechanising sugar production resulted in
higher levels of minimum production and brought beneficial macro-
economic effects by freeing labour for other sectors, increasing internal
demand and diversifying the economic structure, such as developing other
types of agriculture, construction (for housing, health and education programmes) and light industry. At the same time, however, the battle to
'dominate sugar' was only partly won by the end of the 1970s – dependence
on sugar still remained the major engine of, and at the same time, constraint
on, growth. Domestic economic activity exhibited a cyclical pattern heavily
dependent on the availability of (sugar-derived) foreign exchange. The
strategy also embodied heavy political and economic reliance on the Soviet
Union and, as a result of diversifying external economic ties through the
decade, there was a trend towards a higher level of indebtedness to capitalist
trading partners. Indeed, during 1979 to 1982, the problem of external (hard
currency) debts intensified to a critical level, forcing the Cuban government
to request rescheduling arrangements [Banco Nacional de Cuba: 1982].

Countries which are in the early stages of developing strategies of socialist
industrialisation in the bleak conditions of the 1980s face even tighter
constraints. A country such as Ethiopia, for example, has a severe foreign
exchange constraint, and low level of domestic savings, a super-abundant
labour force and limited opportunities for foreign aid. It would seem to have
little option but to adopt a strategy of 'snail's pace' industrialisation (to use

Bukharin's term), which rests on prior development of agriculture to generate foreign exchange and swell the domestic market for manufactures,
favouring labour-intensive branches of industry which provide basic consumer goods and process agricultural produce. The classical 'big push' into
heavy industry seems irrelevant in such circumstances.

Socialist industrialisation in such 'peripheral' conditions, then, calls for
fundamental rethinking. In terms of domestic strategy, the ideas of Mao
Zedong [1956] and of Bukharin during the Soviet industrialisation debate of
the 1920s become very relevant. Mao drew attention to the complementarity
of heavy industry, light industry and agriculture and the costs of allowing one
sector to outrun the others. Bukharin stressed the importance of prior
accumulation in the rural sector as a precondition for industrialisation and
the dynamic role of consumer demand in stimulating industrial growth
[Erlich, 1967]. Bukharin may have lost the argument in the 1920s but he may
yet win it in the 1980s.

On the international aspect, there has been a need for basic rethinking at
both theoretical and policy levels. Classical models of socialist accumulation
have tended to regard foreign trade as relatively marginal. As the Hungarian
economist Köves has argued, in the classical Soviet paradigm, 'self-
sufficiency was the creed of economic policy and the opportunity to establish
a division of labour with non-socialist countries was disregarded in determining the goals and trends of economic development' [Köves: 1981, 114].
During the 1970s socialist economists have increasingly stressed both the
necessity for and the benefits of greater involvement in the global economy
[cf. Chinese theorists Yuan et al: 1980] and the need to move away from
traditional import substitution to export promotion policies. This rethinking
in the more 'mature' socialist context has clear relevance for their successors
in the Third World.

One important recent analytical step forward is the work of Fitzgerald
[1982] who has attempted to develop a model of 'peripheral socialist' accumulation, drawing on Kalecki's economic theory and on his own practical
involvement in Nicaraguan economic planning. Fitzgerald replaces the traditional two-sector model (producer goods and consumer goods) with a
three-sector economy, namely producer goods (I), non-basic consumer
goods (II) and basic consumer goods (III). In a peripheral socialist economy
(PSE) the nature of sector I is distinctive: 'It is the foreign trade sector
which, through exports of primary products at exogenous international
prices, provides ... producer goods, and thus the "heavy industry" of such
"incomplete" economies' [1982: 4]. In many cases, this sector is in fact
agriculture which also, as sector II, provides basic wage goods. This PSE
model is complex and an exegesis is beyond the scope of this paper – the
reader is referred to Fitzgerald's work. But this theoretical reformulation,
with its central focus on foreign trade and agriculture, has important implications for the practical role of socialist developmental states, as we shall see in
the next section.

To summarise this section, we can identify two 'strata' of Third World
socialist industrialisers. The first stratum contains more 'mature' cases such
as China and North Korea where import-substituting strategies have been

successful in establishing an industrial base. The second stratum contains more recently established revolutionary socialist regimes in countries still at the stage of 'proto-industrialisation'.* Each group shares a common international environment but faces distinct sets of problems which have major implications for the character and action of the socialist state. We turn to these questions in the last section.

III: THE CHANGING ROLE OF THE SOCIALIST INDUSTRIALISING STATE

(i) The Role of the Socialist State in Industrialised and Semi-Industrialised Contexts

Let us take our 'mature' economies first. Their experience suggests that pervasive intervention can (given certain basic preconditions) be very productive in the initial stages of industrialisation (in raising levels of accumulation, mobilising and concentrating scarce resources, defining and directing key changes in the industrial structure, regulating international relationships, generating political support and establishing a favourable 'social structure of accumulation'). But the increasingly costly limitations of extensive growth and import substitution create pressures for a basic revision of the relationship between state and economy. The economic reform programmes which have appeared with illuminating consistency in different countries have tried to confront these problems.

In the area of industrial planning and management, reformers have identified the traditional system of centralised planning and administrative management as an increasing impediment to micro-economic efficiency and technological dynamism. They have called for change on three fronts. First, they have argued for the *decentralisation* of economic decision-making, either within the state apparatus (from central to local levels) or from the state apparatus as a whole to industrial production units, both state and collectively owned (for a discussion of these different forms of decentralisation in the Chinese case, see Schurmann [*1968: 195-210*]).

Second, they have stressed the need to shift from pervasive to parametric methods of regulating industrial processes (in terms of current socialist economic terminology, the shift from 'administrative' to 'economic' methods), the latter involving the use of 'economic levers' such as tax, credit, subsidy, etc. Third, they have attempted to increase the role of price mechanisms (the 'law of value') and construct a complementary relationship between planning and (domestic and international) markets.

In essence, these reform proposals envisage a 'roll-back' of the pervasive socialist state. Although, in the conventional socialist debates, these issues tend to be couched in narrowly economic and technocratic terms, their (implicit) political significance is obvious. Moreover, the problems they expose are not merely technical or economic – they are 'structural' in the

*Neither Cuba nor Vietnam fit easily into these broad categories. In terms of its longevity and developmental performance, Cuba is perhaps an intermediate case; Vietnam, though a relatively long-standing socialist regime, has been prevented from following any consistent development path by three decades of war.

sense that they reflect the changing constellation of social forces and distribution of political power in socialist NICs or the industrialised countries of Eastern Europe. Specifically, there are underlying changes in the social character of the state and the nature of countervailing forces in civil society.

The issues raised by economic reformers embody a clash between 'political logic' and 'economic logic'. Just as the former reflects a .veritable Manhattan of skyscraper state organisations, the latter is not some disembodied rationality but rooted in the concrete material interests and socio–political aspirations of rising strata (including technical and professional cadres, the urban working class, certain segments of the rural population and consumers generally). To the extent that the issues are structural, moreover, they are only partially susceptible to 'rational decision-making' or 'policy analysis'; to the extent that the problems they reflect impose increasing constraints on industrial progress, they represent a crisis in the very structure of state socialist societies.

In part, these contradictions in the developmental role of a socialist state reflect a process by which it comes to act 'for itself', to represent apparatchik rather than worker–peasant interests, with negative consequences for both development and socialism. The transformation of the social nature of the state not only impedes economic decentralisation and marketisation; it impresses an indelible stamp on development strategy. The link between state and industrialisation may become pathological – the interests and continued well-being of the state stratum become entwined with the continuation of rapid industrialisation and high levels of accumulation. Thereby it maintains or reinforces a 'state-biased' pattern of development which stresses industry over agriculture, production over exchange and services, producer over consumer goods, large-scale and high-technology industry over small-scale and intermediate technology, state over collective industry and 'self-reliance' over international ties. This can distort development priorities, skew income distribution and perpetuate authoritarian forms of economic management (for the notion of 'state bias', see Nolan and White [1984]). It also impedes a necessary process of overall democratisation in society which, as Brus argues [1973: esp. Chap. 6] becomes not only politically desirable but also economically essential as industrialisation reaches higher stages, as an underpinning for technological creativity, structural flexibility and effective planning.

There is a kind of 'Catch 22' situation operating here: a pervasive state is established in the initial stages of industrialisation for defensible (yet contestable) reasons but then outstays its historical welcome as a bastion of economic irrationality and political authoritarianism. To what extent is this process ineluctable? The historical terrain for countervailing struggle varies: the degree of congelation of self-serving state power varies as does the identity of countervailing political forces (compare the social origins of the Chinese Cultural Revolution, sponsored by a section of the highest state leadership, and the working-class origins of Polish Solidarity). In the older socialist developing countries, debate and struggle tend to arise after the mould has set: in China, the 'radical' initiatives of the Cultural Revolution in the late 1960s, and the 'liberal' reforms of the late 1970s both took on a

well-entrenched state machine and found thoroughgoing change very difficult where not impossible. The Vietnamese economic reforms introduced
after the Sixth Plenum of the Party Central Committee in 1979, which
attacked 'the simple mentality of wanting all production and distribution to
be taken in hand by administrative laws and regulations' [*C. White, 1983:
259*], faced similar constraints. In Cuba, the frenetic mass mobilisations of
the 1960s were accompanied by a proliferating government bureaucracy
which threatened the democratic aspirations of the Cuban revolution and
created an overcentralised and economically inefficient system of planning
and management. During the 1970s, the leadership sponsored moves
towards political democratisation and economic decentralisation – but these
clashed with the bureaucratic heritage of the 1960s and the outcome is
unclear as yet [*Carciofi, 1983: 223-27*].

Historical experience from Eastern Europe and older socialist countries
in the Third World suggests several conclusions: first, economic and political
reform programmes both face formidable obstacles from entrenched state
elites; second, of these two areas of state reform, economic decentralisation,
even of a fairly basic kind (Yugoslavia and Hungary) can be achieved in
certain conditions [*Ardalan, 1980: Balassa, 1978*]; third, political democratisation has proven particularly intractable (witness the continuing political
authoritarianism in Yugoslavia and Hungary).

Semi-industrialised and industrialised socialist nations face a dilemma:
quite apart from the intrinsic importance of economic and political decentralisation as an essential part of genuinely *socialist* development, to survive
and flourish as industrial nations in a global economy still dominated by
capitalist powers, they *must* undergo structural change or face stagnation or
decline. The key to this process would seem to be an increasing appropria-
tion of economic and political power by non-state actors, co-ordination by
regulated markets, a democratised planning system, and an increasingly
parametric state.

(ii) The Socialist State and Proto-Industrialisation

Turning to our second stratum, of 'proto-industrialising' or 'peripheral
socialist' countries, one can argue that certain central dimensions of pervasive state intervention are still historically defensible in the conditions of the
1980s: establishment of an overall planning framework, selective regulation
of external economic ties, decisive action to influence the generation of
savings and allocation of productive investments, direct management of key
nascent industrial sectors, systematic political mobilisation of support for
economic programmes and redistribution of power between social classes as
a precondition for a relatively egalitarian pattern of development.

But the characteristic conditions of peripheral socialist economies must
give rise to considerable sobriety about the limits of pervasive state involvement in managing development. As Fitzgerald has pointed out, states in
such contexts are caught in a vice between two unmanageable sectors: the
international economy which is impossible to plan and (often predominantly
peasant) agriculture which is very difficult to plan administratively. The

consequence is that 'central aspects of economic strategy must ... be the management of commercial relationships' [*1982: 21*]. This implies greater use of parametric methods. In the case of Mozambican agriculture, for example, MacKintosh [*1983*] has made a strong case for the need to integrate state planning with market regulation through flexible price policies. The logic of the PSE also implies a relatively limited, carefully selected state sector, in both industry and agriculture, with considerable autonomy guaranteed to productive units to enable them to cope effectively with the fluctuating demands of internal and external markets. It also requires greater emphasis on non-state forms of ownership, notably on relatively autonomous co-operative or collective enterprises in commerce, industry and agriculture.

CONCLUSION

Developmental choice and flexibility in the adoption of state forms in both strata of socialist industrialisers is heavily dependent on favourable international circumstances. But the conditions of the 1980s are far from favourable. To the extent that Third World socialist countries and the Third World are moving towards greater integration with and dependence on the global economy, they suffer from the consequences of the world economic crisis. While they share many problems in common with their non-socialist counterparts, many face the extra burden of the new cold war – hostile external pressures, whether from the United States in the case of Cuba, Grenada and Nicaragua, or South Africa in the case of Angola or Mozambique. Military pressures of this kind pre-empt discussions about economically and socially advisable development strategies (at the expense of the light industrial and agricultural sectors and of consumption generally), or forms of state involvement. Debates increasingly focus less on the desirable and more on what is possible in a decision-making desert. Although countervailing assistance and opportunities are available from links with the Soviet bloc, these have proven inadequate on various grounds (unacceptable conditionalities, lack of political commitment or technico-economic capacities in the East) and have dwindled as Eastern countries have themselves become embroiled in the international crisis.

If this combination of unfavourable circumstances persists throughout the decade, the prospects for socialist industrialisers are highly problematic. The proto-industrialising countries will find it hard to get the virtuous circles of export-orientated industrialisation moving and the semi-industrialised countries will find further expansion blocked by restricted market access and financial constraints. Such conditions will heighten the central dilemma of socialist developmental states. On the one hand, if they are increasingly thrown back on to themselves, pressured into a strategy of self-reliance through circumstance not choice, they have certain advantages. As a particular form of political economy, they have demonstrated a strong capacity to mobilise and direct social, economic and political resources effectively in response to adversity and limited developmental options. But to maintain the momentum and raise the efficacy of state-sponsored industrialisation, particularly in the more 'mature' cases, requires basic changes in the relationship between state and economy – towards decentralisation, democratisation, parametric regulation and increased use of markets. Moves towards more effective international co-operation between socialist countries might also prove beneficial. On the other hand, external pressure and internal austerity strengthen the rationale for authoritarian controls and increase the likelihood of 'Catch 22' states, which may obstruct the strategic flexibility, organisational adaptability and technology dynamism so necessary to successful industrialisation. The dilemma is profound, the issues are 'structural' and the parameters of choice are narrow indeed. If the dilemma can be solved, the momentum of successful socialist industrialisation, visible over the past four decades, can be maintained. If not, socialist states run the risk of being left behind by more dynamic capitalist competitors, both industrialised (notably Japan) and semi-industrialised (notably the East Asian NICs).

REFERENCES

Alavi, H., 1972, 'The State in Post-Colonial Societies: Pakistan and Bangladesh', *New Left Review*, 74, July-August.
Amsden, A.H., 1979, 'Taiwan's Economic History: A Case of Etatisme and a Challenge to Dependency Theory', *Modern China*, Vol. 5, No. 3, pp. 341-80.
Ardalan, C., 1983, 'Workers' Self-Management and Planning: The Yugoslav Case', *World Development*, Vol. 8, pp. 623-38.
Balassa, B., 1978, 'The Economic Reform in Hungary: Ten Years After', *European Economic Review*, Vol. 11, pp. 245-68.
Banco Nacional de Cuba, 1982, *Economic Report*, Havana, August.
Bennett, D. and K. Sharpe, 'The State as Banker and Entrepreneur: The Last-Resort Character of the Mexican State's Economic Intervention, 1917–76', *Comparative Politics*, Vol. 12, No. 2, pp. 165-89.
Bienefeld, M. and M. Godfrey, (eds.), 1982, 'Introduction' to *The Struggle for Development: National Strategies in an International Context*, New York: John Wiley, pp. 1-24.
Brus, W., 1973, *The Economics and Politics of Socialism*, London: Routledge & Kegan Paul.
Cairncross, A., 1976, 'The Market and the State', in T. Wilson and A. Skinner (eds.), *The Market and the State: Essays in Honour of Adam Smith*, Oxford: Oxford University Press.
Carciofi, R., 1983, 'Cuba in the Seventies', in White, Murray and White (eds.), op.cit., pp. 193-233.
Cardoso, F.H., 1979, 'Capitalist development and the State: bases and alternatives', in Cardoso and E. Faletto, *Dependency and Development in Latin America*, Berkeley: University of California Press, pp. 199-216.
Chung, J.S-h., 1974, *The North Korean Economy: Structure and Development*, Stanford, CA: Hoover Institution.
Debray, R., 1977, 'Marxism and the National Question', *New Left Review*, 105, Sept.-Oct., pp. 25-41.
Ellman, M., 1975, 'Did the Agricultural Surplus Provide the Resources for the Increase in Investment in the USSR During the First Five-Year Plan?', *The Economic Journal*, Vol. 85, pp. 844-64.
Ellman, M., 1979, *Socialist Planning*, Cambridge: Cambridge University Press.
Erlich, A., 1967, *The Soviet Industrialisation Debate 1924–28*, Cambridge, MA: Harvard University Press.
Evans, D. and Alizadeh, P., 1984, 'Trade, Industrialisation and the Visible Hand', *Journal of Development Studies*, (Special Issue) (this volume).
Far Eastern Economic Review, 1983, *Asia 1983 Yearbook*, Hong Kong.
Fitzgerald, E.V.K., 1982, 'The Problem of Balance in the Peripheral Socialist Economy'

(November), Institute of Social Studies, The Hague, mimeo, forthcoming, in K. Martin, *Readings in Capitalist and Non-Capitalist Development Strategies*, London: Heinemann.

Gerschenkron, A., 1966, *Economic Backwardness in Historical Perspective*, Cambridge, MA: Harvard University Press.

Goulbourne, H., 1979, (ed.), *Politics and State in the Third World*, London: Macmillan.

Green, R.H., 1974, 'The Role of the State as an Agent of Economic and Social Development in the Least Developed Countries', *Journal of Development Planning*, No. 6, pp. 1-40.

Halliday, J., 1983, 'The North Korean Enigma', in White, Murray and White, op.cit., pp. 114-54.

Huntington, S.P., 1968, *Political Order in Changing Societies*, New Haven: Yale University Press.

Ikonnicoff, M., 1983, (ed.), 'Le role de l'Etat dans le Tiers Monde', *Tiers-Monde*, Paris, Vol. XXIV, No. 93, January-March.

Kalecki, M., 1967, 'Observations on Social and Economic Aspects of Intermediate Regimes', in *Essays on Developing Countries*, New Jersey: Humanities Press, pp. 30-39.

Köves, A., 1981, 'Socialist Economy and the World Economy', *Review*, Vol. V, No. 1, Summer, pp. 113-33.

Kraus, Willy, 1982, *Economic Development and Social Change in the PRC*, New York: Springer–Verlag.

Lal, Deepak, 1983, *The Poverty of 'Development Economics'*, London: Institute of Economic Affairs.

Lane, D., 1974, 'Leninism as an Ideology of Soviet Development' in E. de Kadt and G. Williams (eds.), *Sociology and Development*, London: Tavistock.

Little, I.M.D., 1979, 'The Experience and Causes of Rapid Labour – Intensive Development in Korea, Taiwan, Hong Kong and Singapore: And the Possibilities of Emulation', ILO/ Artep.

MacKintosh, 1983, 'Agricultural Price Policies in Support of Agrarian Transformation in Centrally Planned Economies in Africa', paper at the FAO Workshop on Transformation of Agrarian Systems in Centrally Planned Economies in Africa, Arusha, Tanzania (October).

Mao Zedong, 1956, 'On the Ten Great Relationships', in his *Selected Works*, Peking, Vol. V, 1977, pp. 284-307.

Meillassoux, C., 1970, 'A Class Analysis of the Bureaucratic Process in Mali', *Journal of Development Studies*, Vol. 6, No. 2, January.

Murray, R., 1975, 'The Internationalization of Capital and the Nation-State', in Hugo Radice (ed.), *International Firms and Modern Imperialism*, Harmondsworth: Penguin, pp. 107-34.

Myrdal, G., 1970, 'The "Soft State" in Underdeveloped Countries', in Paul Streeten (ed.), *Unfashionable Economics*, London: Weidenfeld & Nicolson, pp. 227-42.

Nolan, P. and White, G., 1984, 'Urban Bias, Rural Bias or State Bias? Urban-Rural Relations in Post-Revolutionary China', *Journal of Development Studies*, Vol. 20, No. 3, (Special Issue).

Nove, A., 1983, *The Economics of Feasible Socialism*, London: Allen and Unwin.

Petras, J., 1977, 'State capitalism and the Third World', *Development and Change*, Vol. 8, No. 1, pp. 1-17.

Ranis, G., 1974, 'Employment, Equity and Growth: Lessons from the Philippines Employment Mission', *International Labour Review*, 110, No. 1, July.

Ranis, G., 1982, 'The NICs, the Near-NICs and the World Economy', paper presented in a seminar at the Institute of Development Studies, University of Sussex, 1983, mimeo.

Saul, J.S., 1979, 'The State in Post-Colonial Societies: Tanzania', in H. Goulbourne (ed.), op.cit., pp. 70-91.

Schmitter, P.C. and Lehmbruch, G., 1980, *Trends Towards Corporatist Intermediation*, London: Sage.

Schurmann, F., 1968, *Ideology and Organization in Communist China*, Berkeley CA: University of California Press.

Shivji, I.G., 1975, *Class Struggles in Tanzania*, Dar-es-Salaam: Tanzania Publishing House.

Skocpol, T., 1979, *States and Social Revolutions*, Cambridge: Cambridge University Press.

Smith, B. and Wood, G., 1982, 'State Intervention and Bureaucratic Reproduction: A Comparative Analysis', paper at Political Studies Association Conference, Canterbury, mimeo.

Sutcliffe, R.B., 1971, *Industry and Underdevelopment*, London: Addison-Wesley.

Szostak, M., 1983, 'Le secteur public dans les pays du tiers monde: sa formation, son expansion', *Tiers Monde*, Vol. XXIV: No. 93, pp. 53-74.

UNIDO, 1979, *World Industry since 1960: Progress and Prospects* (Special Issue of the Industrial Development Survey for the Third General Conference of UNIDO), New York: UNIDO.

White, C., 1983, 'Recent Debates in Vietnamese Development Policy', in White, Murray and White, op. cit., pp. 234-70.

White, G., 1982, 'North Korean Juche: The Political Economy of Self-Reliance', in Bienefeld and Godfrey, op. cit., pp. 323-54.

White, G., 1983a, 'The Post-Revolutionary Chinese State', in Victor Nee and David Mozingo (eds.), *State and Society in Contemporary China*, Cornell University Press, pp. 27-52.

White, G., 1983b, 'Revolutionary Socialist Development in the Third World: An Overview', in G. White *et al.*, op. cit., pp. 1-34.

White, G., Murray, R., and White, C. (eds.), 1983, *Revolutionary Socialist Development in the Third World*, Brighton: Wheatsheaf Books.

Wilczynski, J., 1972, *Socialist Economic Development and Reforms*, London: Macmillan.

World Bank, 1983, *World Development Report 1983*, Oxford: Oxford University Press.

Yuan Wenqi, Dai Lunzhang and Wang Linsheng, 1980, 'International Division of Labour and China's Economic Relations with Foreign Countries', *Social Sciences in China*, No. 1.

Industry and Underdevelopment Re-examined*

by Bob Sutcliffe

Recent work by Lipton, Stewart, Warren and others has, from differing standpoints, called into question much of the conventional wisdom of the dependency school (shared by my book Industry and Underdevelopment*) about the relationship between development and industrialisation. Four of these arguments – that industrialisation is necessary to meet human needs, that underdeveloped countries are in general not succeeding in industrialising, that capital-intensive technology is desirable and that industrialisation requires more autarky – are re-examined. They are all found to be in need of considerable modification; but the general lines of the proferred alternatives to them are for the most part not accepted either. Part of the problem is diagnosed as insufficient concern for the human consequences of 'actually existing industrialisations' and too nationalistic a conception of socialism.*

I

In my book entitled *Industry and Underdevelopment*, written for the most part fifteen years ago, I argued the following positions:

I: that the industrialisation of countries was (according both to pure theory and to historical experience) necessary to eliminate human poverty and satisfy human needs with rising standards of living; only a small number of areas or countries could, due to super-generous natural endowments, escape this logic;

II: that up to the present only a privileged few countries had industrialised successfully, and that it did not look from the evidence as if the underdeveloped countries were undergoing the process at all, or at best they were undergoing it at a very slow pace;

III: that successful modern industrialisation in general requires the use of large-scale units of production to take advantage of economies of scale; and also the use of modern technology which usually means relatively capital-intensive techniques. This is one of the advantages of being a latecomer. Nonetheless many qualifications to this were made and a cautious welcome was given to certain versions of intermediate technology and forms of technological dualism;

* School of Economics and Politics, Kingston Polytechnic. I am grateful to other contributors to this volume for comments on an earlier draft, especially to the editors, to David Evans and to Martin Bell; and to Kaighn Smith for help with the numbers.

IV: that because there was something in the existence of, or policies of, industrialised countries which prevented the independent industrialisation of the underdeveloped ones, such a process was only possible if these latter could immunise themselves against the damaging effects of contact with the industrialised countries; and this, with many qualifications, suggested the need for a fairly high degree of economic autarky which quite possibly could only be achieved through socialism in the underdeveloped countries; this was combined with a generally positive evaluation of the economic aspects of the Soviet, and often also the Chinese, model of industrialisation.

These positions, I think, coincide with or overlap a range of positions which have become a kind of orthodoxy throughout a large part of the development economics profession, especially on the socialist and nationalist left. This orthodoxy includes various theories which have come to be known under the collective title of 'dependency theory'.

All these ideas have been more widely discussed during the period since I did the reading for my book. Now, on reflection, I find that just about all of them require at least a good deal of critical modification, and some of them more of a thoroughgoing revision. In this article I will briefly explain why, referring to a number of the more controversial and interesting writings on the subject in the last few years. These include: Michael Lipton's *Why Poor People Stay Poor*; Fritz Schumacher's *Small is Beautiful*; Frances Stewart's *Technology and Underdevelopment*; Arghiri Emmanuel's *Intermediate or Underdeveloped Technology?*; Gavin Kitching's *Development and Underdevelopment in Historical Perspective*, and Bill Warren's *Imperialism, Pioneer of Capitalism*. All of these are works which have in some way managed to have an impact on discussion within the field of development economics by changing the terms of the existing debate. They have all, therefore, forced economists working in the field of development to re-examine old positions.

II

Gavin Kitching's stimulating book gives a good summary of the traditional and almost universally accepted argument for industrialisation as a necessary step towards the elimination of human poverty. It is based on the expanding variety of human needs as material standards rise, and as such it is incontestable, almost axiomatic. But, more than before, I think it needs some quite strong qualifications.

The argument is a theoretical one. It assumes that more or less any conceivable evolution of consumption preferences for some distance above the mere subsistence level of income involves a rising share of industrial goods. In principle, it could be objected, these goods could be supplied for any given population by the production and exchange of other non-industrial goods and services as long as the levels of productivity and the terms of trade of the non-industrial sectors allow it. In other words, in principle a nation of bee-keepers, or of bankers, or of masseurs, or of airline pilots could have a high standard of living. And of course non-industrial workers in industrialised countries often do have a high standard of living.

That there should be a whole nation of such people, however, is scarcely possible – it could occur only for small countries extraordinarily well endowed by nature. In any case, for one nation to live like that implies industrialisation somewhere else to provide inputs to the primary production or services. So this whole line of argument is not really one against industrialisation in general, only in some very special places.

Another objection to the standard pro-industrialisation argument is less often made but is, in my view, much more important. The theoretical argument for industrialisation as a route to satisfying human needs does not prove that real historical or present-day industrialisations in fact do supply human needs well. Conceivable ideal industrialisation will satisfy needs; but 'actually existing industrialisation' (to adapt a phrase of Rudolph Bahro) may not. And I contend that in most cases it does not.

It is surely a fact that the standard, universally accepted *theoretical* defence of industrialisation has never been the main motive for any actually existing industrialisation. Real-world industrialisations have not been motivated directly by the desire to satisfy human needs in general. In cases where industrialisation has been fostered by state authorities then this has usually been done as a means of increasing the military might of the nation against others, or to augment the power of the ruling group within their own country. Hence a very great part of industrial output during the process of industrialisation has taken the form of goods which in no way meet human needs but rather create the means to destroy or intimidate human beings.

Also, even if the irreducible nature of human tastes dictates a high proportion of industrial output it does not follow that either the total amount of industrial goods which have been produced, or their composition between different products, are consonant with satisfying human needs. In other words some very radically different structure of industrialisation might in principle have met human needs better. No doubt it is reaction against the deficiencies of actually existing industrialisation which has partly fuelled the popular argument for 'basic needs' strategies; and some of these are very rejecting of industrialisation in a way that I do not intend to be.

The frequent non-congruence in practice between actual industrial output and the fulfilment of human needs illustrates one way in which important truths can be obscured by economists' excessive concentration on industrialisation as a process in the life of *nations* (the abstract) rather than of *people* (the concrete)). Another problem with this national emphasis is geographical. Even in the most industrialised of nations there are areas of economic backwardness where industrialisation and its effects have not penetrated. Usually, of course, in the industrialised countries there are no longer large numbers of people living in 'pre-industrial conditions' in those areas because the original inhabitants have long since migrated to the more industrialised areas (urbanisation). Historically, too, industrialisation was accompanied by another form of migration – international migration from the slower or non-industrialising areas to the faster industrialising areas – particularly of course from Europe to North America. This form of migration has – for racist and other reasons – become much more difficult in the modern epoch. Therefore international migration is now largely ruled out as

a method of spreading the 'benefits' of industrialisation to a wider proportion of the world's population. This is perhaps one reason why it does make
some sense to emphasise the polarisation of developed/industrialised and
underdeveloped/non-industrialised areas today as a polarisation of *nations*
rather than as one of the forms of intra-national polarisation which have
been common to all industrialisations.

On the other hand, to see the polarisation between nations as the main
and invariable feature of modern economic change can be extremely misleading. It passes over the fact that some industrial growth has taken place in
the underdeveloped countries and that important processes of polarisation
have been taking place within them; and this is related to patterns of world
industrial growth which, because of the growing internationalisation of the
capitalist economy, are less comprehensible in terms of nations than they
were in the past.

The dependency/national polarisation approach used to be taken to imply
that all nations as at present constituted ought, if they want to enrich
themselves to European levels, to undergo a parallel process of national
industrialisaion. At best this argument could only apply to broad *regions*
since, although the economies of scale argument is often taken much too far,
there are enough technical economies of scale to mean that it is inconsistent
for very small nations (of which there are very many in the Third World)
both to want to enrich themselves and to want to undergo a complete
industrialisation within their own borders. It is almost certain, and no longer
widely denied, that some processes of industrialisation which have actually
occurred (measured in terms of the composition of GDP and so on) behind
high tariff walls have led not to national enrichment but to some national
impoverishment. Political decentralisation in general seems to me to be
desirable, but not with every decentralised unit aiming to construct an
industrial replica of the superstates within its own borders.

The most ardent proponents of rapid industrialisation will often admit
that actually existing industrialisations may leave something to be desired in
their meeting of human needs; but, they argue, at any event they have
created the *potential* for those needs to be met more effectively. This
argument is related, I think, to the question of the relative valuation of the
consumption of different generations. It tends to value the consumption of
future generations highly relative to the present one (and the present one
highly relative to past ones). Even in general philosophical terms this
balance of interest would be hard to justify to those whose needs are not met
today. It can only be defended by arguing that to ignore the interests of the
unborn will (by storing up crisis and disaster) in fact cause more long-run
suffering for the living than valuing their consumption relatively low. But in
any event such decisions are never in the real world taken by society as a
whole according to rational philosophical argument. They are taken by
ruling classes and elites (often assisted by economists and other intellec-
tuals). And those who are relatively privileged today will be likely to act as if
they value the consumption of future generations more than the consumption of present ones (themselves excepted). Those who starve today would
no doubt evaluate differently. But by definition they do not have the power.

Of course it can be argued, again theoretically, that it is possible to conceive a rapid industrialisation and the restriction of today's consumption taking place in a much more egalitarian manner than they have in practice. Thus high levels of investment *could* be financed with less poverty and deprivation today. (In general terms this is the argument associated with the left opposition in the Soviet industrialisation debate.) This is correct in theory, but there is no example of it in practice, which suggests that the political conditions for it are at very best extremely difficult to attain and may be altogether unattainable [*Skouras, 1977*]. If the inevitable political concomitants of rapid industrialisation are what has been observed then this is surely an argument if not for less rapid industrialisation then at least against the adventuristic industrialisation targets so beloved of planning bureaucrats and politicians.

To sum up, a theoretical argument for industrialisation based on human need is obviously valid in theory. But it is not proved by existing or past industrialisations. Most people involved in the theoretical discussion can see themselves as beneficiaries of past industrialisations. But more knowledge of the costs paid by the victims of all the capitalist and non-capitalist industrialisations of the past ought to make us very wary of the application of the theoretical argument to industrialisation in the present. Economists should therefore devote more attention to the quality of industrialisations as they affect the lives of living human beings. So far industrialisation has been more historically progressive in theory than in practice.

III

Although I shall not keep alluding to them, the points made in the previous section have some relevance to evaluating the quantitative data on the recent industrialisation of underdeveloped countries. I accept that the available evidence on this suggests a faster rate of industrial growth in the underdeveloped countries than I had expected at the time of writing *Industry and Underdevelopment*.

According to the World Bank statisticians, the aggregate rate of growth of both industrial and manufacturing output have been over three per cent a year for 34 low-income countries and over six per cent a year for 59 middle-income countries over the two decades 1960–81 [*World Bank, 1983*]. These rates have been higher than for the industrialised capitalist countries and so the share of the underdeveloped countries in the world's manufacturing output (excluding high-income oil producers and East European planned economies) has risen a little – from 17.6 per cent in 1960 to 18.9 per cent in 1981 (calculated from World Bank [*1983*]). Their share of world exports of manufactures rose from 3.9 per cent to 8.2 per cent in the same period. To view this slightly differently the developing countries' share of the manufactured imports of all industrial countries rose from 5.3 per cent in 1962 to 13.1 per cent in 1978 [*World Bank, 1982*]. According to the World Bank figures, the share of the GDP of low-income countries arising in the industrial sector rose from 25 per cent in 1960 to 34 per cent in 1981. For manufacturing the rise was only from 11 to 16 per cent. The record is much more modest for this group if India and China are omitted (and it is China which really makes the difference). For the remaining countries the share of industry rose from 12 to only 17 per cent; and for manufacturing, from nine to 10 per cent. In the middle-income group the changes were from 30 to 38 per cent for industry, and from 20 to 22 per cent for manufacturing alone [*World Bank, 1983*].

As everyone has to acknowledge, the performance of different countries has varied very much. A very high proportion of the aggregate growth, especially of manufactured exports, has been concentrated in a very few countries indeed (compare Schmitz above). These are the ones generally known as the Newly Industrialised Countries (NICs).

Of course, it is a debatable point how much significance should be attached to this qualification. The optimists argue that the NICs are an *example* which any underdeveloped country could have followed with the right policies. They imply that there is no overall problem of markets for potential competitively produced manufactured exports. Some of those who do acknowlege that the potential market is limited argue that the NICs, through good fortune or good policy, did relatively better than other countries, but do not rule out the possibility that the benefit could be more evenly spread if not much greater in the aggregate. Among the more orthodox pessimists, other than those who seek spuriously to deny the success of the NICs, most regard them as *exceptions* to the general failure of the underdeveloped countries to industrialise. There has certainly been some polarisation between the NICs and other developing countries, even though this phenomenon may not be as clear as is often supposed, since there are some near-NICs and not-so-near-NICs.

Despite the NICs there is little evidence that more than a handful of countries have in the last two or three decades been passing through an equivalent process of industrialisation to that which transformed the structure of society and the level of labour productivity in, say, nineteenth-century Europe or twentieth-century Japan.

Such a qualititative structural change is of course hard to measure. But it was some approximation to it which I was trying to achieve by proposing in *Industry and Underdevelopment* a multi-dimensional definition of an industrialised country. It would be only honest to admit that I started from a preconception about which countries could be regarded as industrialised and which could not. I then looked for a quantitative basis for the presupposed qualitative difference between these two classes of countries. The 'test' of industrialisation I arrived at was a three-part one: industrialised countries were defined as those with 25 per cent or more of GDP in the industrial sector; with 60 per cent of industrial ouput in manufacturing; and with 10 per cent of the population employed in industrial activities. The reasons for this definition are not worth repeating here. I reiterate it because I want to look at the results which would be obtained by applying the same 'tests' today (most of the figures used in the book were from the mid-1960s) [*Sutcliffe, 1971: 16-26*].

Under the definition the countries which were 'industrialised' at the time of writing *Industry and Underdevelopment* were the expected countries of

Western Europe, Eastern Europe, North America, Japan and Australasia with the addition of Argentina, Hong Kong and Malta. No doubt Singapore would have figured in them too had I been able to obtain the appropriate figures. On the borderline were Uruguay, Israel, Yugoslavia and Portugal.

Since then, according to the latest figures, all the borderline cases have crossed the line and are now industrialised according to these criteria. The only countries to have passed the combined test since then are South Korea and probably Taiwan. An examination of other candidates, including NICs and near-NICs, suggest that most of them are not even approaching the fulfilment of the three criteria of the definition and this is usually because industrial employment is not expanding as a share of the population, though on the first two criteria alone (the sectoral structure of output) many of them would 'pass'.

I believe that these results call into question some of the optimistic conclusions drawn from the aggregate statistics by writers such as Bill Warren. A number of other statistical points also tend to deepen my scepticism of the 'optimistic' perspective.

First, there remains a vast difference between the level of manufacturing ouput per head of population in the most retarded of the advanced industrialised countries and even the most statistically industrialised of the underdeveloped ones. So while the definitions based on sectoral shares and the labour force show South Korea to be as industrialised as the UK the difference between the two countries' levels of manufacturing ouput per head (1978 figures) is between $621 and $2,667. In a number of Third World countries (of which South Korea is an example) real structural change has been taking place which in relation to the patterns followed historically by the presently advanced industrialised countries is 'premature'.

Part of this may be a statistical illusion due to differences between domestic and world relative prices. But I believe that many countries have in a real sense structurally industrialised at a much lower level of labour productivity than was the case in the advanced countries. Of the NICs only Singapore has a level of manufacturing ouput per head higher than some industrialised countries; and that is an unfair comparison given that Singapore is a city-state without a hinterland or rural sector. Singapore's statistics can prove very little; other individual cities in the Third World might show similar results if they could be statistically isolated from their hinterlands (for example, Sao Paulo).

Second, in a number of cases the noted structural shifts in the composition of ouput are more apparent than real since they result not from a rise in industry so much as a fall in agriculture. In the last 15 years agricultural performance in many underdeveloped countries has been notoriously bad. Out of the World Bank's low-income category 23 out of 33 countries have experienced a decline in food ouput per head during the 1970s [*World Bank, 1982: Table 1*]. This tragic phenomenon produces a pattern of structural change which appears to be the same but in reality differs from that of successfully industrialising countries. 'Industrialisation' here is a sign not of economic advance but of economic decline.

Third, statistics produced by UNIDO suggest another important phenomenon. In aggregate they show a fairly fast rise in industrial output in underdeveloped countries between 1955 and 1979 (around seven per cent, which squares with the World Bank figure). But they also show (in contrast to the received wisdom) that industrial employment has also grown quite fast [*UNIDO, 1982*]. Putting these two figures together, however, does not amount to a double success story because it implies a low increase in industrial productivity – of less than two per cent a year. Yet everyone points to evidence of the adoption of high productivity modern techniques in many industries (and this is in fact widely regarded as a problem in itself). If that is really happening then these aggregate figures imply that some of the remarkably high increase in industrial employment has been in occupations which have extremely low levels of labour productivity.

There could be two reasons for this. One is that the product mix of new employment has been towards relatively low productivity industries. But this is unlikely since the UNIDO figures show that the aggregate figures are replicated in virtually all separate industries. So we cannot conclude that the phenomenon has been due to the unbalanced growth of any particular industry. The other possible reason is that the increase in employment has taken place in low productivity techniques. This may be connected with widespread observations that there is in underdeveloped countries a large sector of very primitive small-scale workshops which are very far from modern factory industry. This is seen by various economists as a form of disguised unemployment, or as part of the 'informal sector'. Again, however, it is hard to believe that this phenomenon, although it surely exists, shows up in aggregate statistics for industrial ouput and employment since statistics for these kinds of activities are notoriously elusive. If they were included in full then the tendency for slow productivity growth in industry would be even more marked; it may even become productivity decline. While a mystery remains, these speculations suggest once again that not all statistical industrialisation represents economic progress in the normally accepted sense.

The available statistics suggest to me that both extremes in the argument over the industrialisation record of the Third World are wrong: both Warren's optimistic view that industrialisation, the equivalent of the process which transformed the advanced countries, is now taking place quite rapidly in the underdeveloped ones; and the orthodox dependency view that hardly anything significant is happening. The truth seems not to be midway between the two but more complex and ambiguous than either. A form of industrialisation has been taking place in quite a widespread manner. But in many countries it is composed of different elements which are not homogeneous and do not unambiguously represent economic modernisation.

In many countries what seems to be happening is that modern industry is growing at high and rising productivity levels and at the same time small-scale, more primitive industry survives at low, possibly declining productivity levels, but provides a meagre living for a growing share of the people. What may be occurring therefore is a process of internal polarisation, one which is more complex and more extreme than I envisaged when writing

Industry and Underdevelopment and one which is very different from what took place in the successful industrialisations of the past.

IV

Heated debates have raged over the last ten years or so about the related questions of choice of techniques, economies of scale, urban bias and so on. On this collection of questions economists have tended to range themselves in two rival camps: those who favour rapid industrial development, extol modern technologies, reject (or ignore) the notion of urban bias and so on; and those who favour rural development, think urban bias has been significant and damaging and favour the use of intermediate (or appropriate) technology. Harking back to earlier debates on related subjects Kitching [*1982*] and Byres [*1979*], have described parts of this discussion as one between populists and anti-populists, the latter by implication being on the side of historical progress, the former being largely backward-looking.

The socialist tradition in the last century has by and large rejected the kinds of arguments which are today produced by such writers as Schumacher and Lipton. Just as Marx and Engels are supposed to have vanquished the Utopian socialists, Lenin defeated the Narodniks and (dare one add?) Stalin triumphed over Bukharin, so today populists are widely seen by socialists as the remnants of a losing tradition. On the whole I think this was the position adopted in my book, though with some reservations. Today I regard those reservations as much more important. But the debate is one which takes place at so many levels that it is hard to disentangle them into some coherent threads.

Socialist orthodoxies usually contain a strong belief in the idea that the use of the most advanced techniques will maximise the surplus and thereby the rate of development, and that such techniques are becoming increasingly large-scale and capital-intensive. However, despite many obstinate attempts to deny it (such as that recently by Emmanuel [*1982*]), there is convincing evidence that in many activities less capital-intensive techniques may be surplus-maximising, that not all technical progress implies growing minimum scale of production, and that better directed research can result in more appropriate techniques [*Stewart, 1978; Kaplinsky, 1982*]. Such newly discovered techniques can sometimes not only be economically and technically efficient but can also possess other virtues.

The choice of techniques debate has seldom broken out of a neo-classical mould. It is usually posed as a discussion about maximising output or the rate of growth of output. So far it has not fully incorporated work on technology which sees the choice of technique as much more than a technical, economic choice. From the point of view of the choosers (whether they be capitalists or state bureaucrats) technological choice is often determined by questions of control and discipline of the labour force within the production process. Machine-paced operations may be chosen not for their superiority in terms of technical efficiency but for their ability to enforce labour discipline. From the point of view of the worker the nature of technology can determine much of the character of her or his life. Of course, many labour-intensive technologies are associated with the most inhuman forms of exploitation and wage slavery. But also many capital-intensive technologies, especially of mass, assembly-line production, are associated with the loss of human independence and control by the worker.

If we are to consider industrialisation not from the point of view of the nation-state or other inhuman abstractions but from the point of view of its relationship with real human beings alive, and to be born, then these points are every bit as important as the ones concerned with the maximising of output and growth (which also of course indirectly affect real people's lives). This is why I think that the populists, intermediate technologists and the like have introduced a crucial set of considerations into the debate on industrialisation.

This does not mean that I agree with all that they say. But I think that it is important for economists to admit that the questions they raise are necessary dimensions to the problems of industrialisation and the choice of technology which are excluded from the usual economists' debate. Unfortunately the reason that they are excluded is that they represent in some form the interests of those who stand to be the victims of the industrialisation process. These are usually the groups in society that do not have an audible voice. When they do the practical choice of technology becomes a different question. The reason, for example, why the level of productivity in the German motor industry is higher than in the British surely has a lot to do with the ability of British workers' trade unions to defend themselves against the consequences of advanced technologies. And it is hard to imagine that Soviet industrialisation would have occurred in anything like the way it has if the political voices of the working class had not been so completely stifled.

I think that the consequences of this argument is that in political systems which are basically exploitative, be they capitalist or 'socialist', the existence of elements of workers' democracy may, by constraining technological choice, slow down the process of industrialisation. But that does not mean that there is a trade-off between democracy and industrialisation, at least not in any simple sense. It is part of the job of economists who are concerned both with democracy and with long-term economic progress to search for ways of transcending this trade-off. One element of this would surely be intermediate technology – not conceived of as a traditional technology designed to preserve traditional ways of life which can be oppressive to those condemned to lead them (especially to women) as more modern forms of tyranny, but rather conceived as modern forms of technology which allow endurable labour processes. This would only make sense in a humane and democratic form of society which hardly exists today anywhere on earth. But that fact does not seem to me to justify economists collaborating in making choices which are only rational in the context of societies in which it is the beneficiaries, and not the victims, of industrialisation who take all the decisions.

There is nevertheless an unsatisfactory aspect to the view of many of the populists and appropriate technologists – their failure to distinguish between different classes of victim in the industrialisation process. Traditional or rural exploiters tend not to be sufficiently distinguished from those whom they exploit today. This can be particularly true of Michael Lipton's [*1977*] notion of urban bias which elides class distinctions within rural (and urban) society as Terry Byres [*1979*] quite convincingly argues. On a different plane, it is worth reminding ourselves that a humane concern for the victims of actually existing industrialisation can easily slip into a defence of pre-industrial privilege and exploitation, an opposition to radical change of any kind, and a defence of the values and modes of life of villages which are so often especially reactionary and oppressive.

It has often been said that it is necessary to accept (for *who* to accept we may ask?) the suffering attendant on processes like industrialisation in the interests of material progress which will pave the way for a better life for future generations. If ever this view was justified it no longer is today. Partly this is because the advanced nature of technology means that (at least if research and development work is radically re-directed) the potential choices are far wider than they were in the nineteenth century. The resources and technology surely now exist to resolve all the principle material problems of humanity. We live in potential affluence; the potential is unrealised for reasons which are basically political.

V

The main source of unease I have tried to draw attention to is the tendency among economists on various sides of the debates about industrialisation to which I have briefly referred, to ignore the problem of the victims. This has been especially evident, I think, in the generally positive evaluation among economists, especially socialists, of the industrialisation of the Soviet Union, a process mainly directed towards increasing the military power under the control of a dictatorial group and one in the course of which millions died or suffered unbelievable torments. Often these things are either passed over; or else there is a rather blithe assumption that somehow all the economic success of the Soviet Union could be repeated without its political aspects. This has generally been the line of those who support the positions of the left opposition on industrialisation during the 1920s debate and after.

I have always believed that in some sense Stalinism held back rather than advanced the development of the Soviet Union by imprisoning the creative human endeavour of the majority of its citizens. But I do not think that means that economically the same process would have been possible in a more humane environment. The kind of nationalist industrialisation which took place in the Soviet Union in some ways required the politics which went with it. A more humane and democratic process could have occurred only in the context of a much more open, less nationalistic and militaristic environment – a fact which supporters of the left opposition then and now have too often forgotten.

The cult of Soviet success has combined with the analysis of dependency theory to produce the notion that the most appropriate road to industrialisation in the Third World today is via a non-capitalist route which would of necessity be relatively autarkic. This was a major theme of *Industry and Underdevelopment* and others have developed it more explicitly. I now believe that it is the wrong way round to look at the relation of socialism and industrialisation. It sees socialism not so much as an end defined in terms of social justice and individual fulfilment, but as a means to effect separation from the international capitalist economy. It becomes a theory of 'socialism in one country' in many countries. Socialism is devalued, as it is in practice so often in the real world, into a euphemism for nationalism and perhaps for dictatorship as well. It loses a central element of the nineteenth-century socialist tradition which is its internationalism – the idea that material and political problems in the world as a whole will only be resolved by a combined struggle of the oppressed in the advanced and the backward parts of the world because their exploiters are internationalised. The internationalism of capitalism was seen in that tradition as something to be built on rather than something to be reversed.

However, the reaction of Warren and others to the deficiencies of nationalist socialism seems to me to be equally wrong. Warren and Emmanual reassert Marx's surely invalidated expectation that capitalism was capable of developing the whole world in the image of the advanced countries and that the working class would then inherit an advanced planet. Just as much as the advocates of the non-capitalist road to industrialisation, such arguments imply a conception of historical progress in which the suffering of victims is seen as inevitable and ultimately justified. Growing inequality can be interpreted as a necessary element in a process of development which would enable the problems of the majority of people to be resolved in the future. Emmanuel argues that:

> if capitalism is hell there exists a still more frightful hell: that of less developed capitalism ... if [capitalist] development does not *ipso facto* lead to the satisfaction of 'social needs', it nonetheless constitutes, via the political struggles made possible by a certain pluralism inherent in the higher phase of the industrial revolution, a much more favourable framework for a certain satisfaction of these needs than those of past class regimes [*Emmanuel, 1982: 105*].

I think that the experience has substantially invalidated these ideas that capitalist development has created and can still create the material preconditions for socialism which requires merely political struggle at the right moment in history (but not yet!) [*Auerbach, 1982*]. The economic structure of advanced capitalism is inappropriate in very many ways as a material basis for a socialist society. It is inappropriate to a very great extent in terms of the products it produces (armaments, far too many motor cars, planned obsolescent goods and so on). It is even more inappropriate in terms of the forms of participation in the labour process possible with the favoured technology (over-centralisation, de-skilling, etc.). It is in many ways a totalitarian, alienating experience which does not create, even destroys, the values which could help to build a truly socialist society. Capitalist development has helped to create a view of socialism which is centralised, statist and bureaucratically controlled from above – a necessary measure until the 'cultural level of the people' can be raised.

I believe that it is at least possible to contemplate a process of economic development and industrialisation in the poor countries which would have less of these deficiencies of actually existing industrialisation, capitalist or 'socialist'. Socialist thinking on these questions needs to recapture some of its Utopian traditions.

As a caste development economists have been a very privileged stratum during the years since 1945. We have found it easy to earn very high salaries and live interesting and even exotic working lives. I do not think that this disentitles us from having views about the world. But it does disentitle us from recommending that the material suffering of anyone alive today should be regarded as acceptable in the interests of the abstraction of human progress. It should oblige us to contribute to the search for a more humane road to economic development than the rocky path represented by actually existing industrialisation.

REFERENCES

Auerbach, Paul, 1982, 'From Menshevism and Post-Revolutionary Adventurism to Stalinism and the New Industrial State', Kingston Polytechnic School of Economics and Politics *Discussion Paper in Political Economy*, No. 39.

Byres, T.J., 1979, 'Of Neo-Populist Pipe-Dreams: Daedalus in the Third World and the Myth of Urban Bias', *Journal of Peasant Studies*, Vol. 6, No. 2.

Emmanuel, A., 1982, *Appropriate or Underdeveloped Technology?*, Chichester: John Wiley.

Kaplinsky, R., 1982, 'Fractions of capital and accumulation in Kenya', Institute of Development Studies, University of Sussex, Brighton, mimeo.

Kitching, Gavin, 1982, *Development and Underdevelopment in Historical Perspective: Populism, Nationalism and Industrialisation*, London and New York: Methuen.

Lipton, Michael, 1977, *Why Poor People Stay Poor: A Study of Urban Bias in World Development*, London: Temple Smith.

Schumacher, E.F., 1973, *Small is Beautiful: Economics as if People Mattered*, New York: Harper & Row.

Singh, Ajit, 1979, 'The "Basic Needs" approach to development *vs.* the New International Economic Order: the significance of Third World industrialisation', *World Development*, Vol. 7, No. 6.

Skouras, Thanos, 1977, 'The Political Concomitants of Rapid Industrialisation' (Thames Papers in Political Economy), Thames Polytechnic, London.

Stewart, Frances, 1978, *Technology and Underdevelopment*, London: Macmillan.

Sutcliffe, R.B., 1972, *Industry and Underdevelopment*, London: Addison Wesley.

UNCTAD, 1978, 'Recent trends and developments in trade in manufactures and semi-manufactures of developing countries and territories: 1977 review'. Report by the UNCTAD Secretariat, Geneva.

UNIDO, 1982, *Yearbook of Industrial Statistics*, Vienna: UNIDO.

Warren, Bill, 1980, *Imperialism: Pioneer of Capitalism*, London: Verso.

World Bank, 1982, *World Development Report*, Washington, D.C.: IBRD.

World Bank, 1983, *World Development Report*, Washington, D.C.: IBRD.